D1393507

THE M. & E. **HANDBOOK** SERIES

LOCAL GOVERNMENT

MICHAEL P. BARBER, LL.B.(Lond.)

Lecturer at Ewell County
Technical College

MACDONALD & EVANS LTD

8 John Street, London, W.C.1

1969

First published September 1969

©

MACDONALD AND EVANS LTD
1969

S.B.N. 7121 1218 9

HANDBOOK *Conditions of Sale*

*Printed in Great Britain by Butler & Tanner, Ltd,
Frome and London*

GENERAL INTRODUCTION

The HANDBOOK Series of Study Notes

HANDBOOKS are designed to help students to prepare and revise for professional and other examinations. The books are carefully programmed so as to be self-contained courses of tuition in the subjects they cover. For this purpose they comprise detailed study notes, practical questions and answers, and hints on examination technique.

HANDBOOKS can be used on their own or in conjunction with recommended textbooks. They are written by technical college lecturers, examiners, and others with wide experience of students' difficulties and requirements. At all stages the main objective of the authors has been to prepare students for the practical business of passing examinations.

P. W. D. REDMOND
General Editor

NOTICE TO LECTURERS

Many lecturers are now using HANDBOOKS as working texts to save time otherwise wasted by students in protracted note-taking. The purpose of the series is to meet practical teaching requirements as far as possible, and lecturers are cordially invited to forward comments or criticisms to the Publishers for consideration.

GENERAL INTRODUCTION

The HANDBOOK Series of Study Notes

HANDBOOKS are designed to help students to prepare and revise for professional and other examinations. The books are carefully paragraphed so as to be self-contained courses of study for the subjects they cover. For this purpose they comprise detailed study notes, graded questions and answers, and hints on examination technique.

HANDBOOKS can be used on their own or in conjunction with recommended textbooks. They are written by technical experts, examiners, and others with wide experience of syllabus, difficulties and requirements. At all stages the authors' objective is to assist students to pass their practical benefits and passing examinations.

R. W. D. Kennard
General Editor

NOTICE TO READERS

Have you ever been using HANDBOOKS as a reference...

AUTHOR'S PREFACE

THE object of the HANDBOOK is to provide a guide to the study of local government in England and Wales which will not only explain the structural and legal aspects of the system, but will also attempt to show the problems facing contemporary local government.

The HANDBOOK is intended principally for students studying for the examinations of the Local Government Examinations Board, which has kindly given permission for the reproduction of its past examination questions. The HANDBOOK is not intended completely to replace textbooks on the subject, and indeed it is doubtful whether any book can completely fill the needs of a student of this complex and ever-changing subject. It is thus confidently expected that students will supplement their studies by experience gained from their employment, especially as regards the practical day-to-day working of the system, and by reading widely. In particular, useful articles appear regularly in the *Municipal Journal*, and from time to time in *New Society*. Emphasis is also to be placed during the present reforming period in local government on the Reports of the Maud and Mallaby Committees, and on the Reports of the Royal Commissions on Local Government.

July 1969   M. P. B.

CONTENTS

CHAPTER I

WHAT IS LOCAL GOVERNMENT?

CENTRAL AND LOCAL GOVERNMENT

1. The basic idea. With the possible exception of the USSR, the successful autocratic state administering all functions of government through direct organs of the central body has not yet been achieved. It is doubted whether a situation involving the complete absence of any local autonomy can be evolved in a democratic state, and indeed, countries in Communist Eastern Europe which have attempted to govern on such a basis have found it necessary to resort to some form of local administration through non-central bodies.

NOTE: The USSR has officially recognised (at least since the Constitution of 1936) the necessity of administering a wide range of functions on a local basis, but has rigorously controlled such local units by the exercise of central power and through the co-ordination of the ubiquitous Communist Party.

2. General characteristics. Some degree of local government characterises every state in the world, and the significant point is not the mere existence of local government but the degree of such local power. Local government means authority to determine and to execute matters within a restricted area inside and smaller than the whole state. The variant, *local self-government*, is important in that it emphasises the freedom of the local unit, to a greater or lesser degree, to decide and act of its own initiative and responsibility.

Local government involves the administering of services on a local basis by local bodies, and in attempting to construct an adequate definition certain basic distinctions must be drawn.

3. Federal and unitary systems. Local government in its true sense is synonymous with *subordinate* government. A federal system involves autonomous divisions of a country joining for a common purpose but retaining varying degrees of independence. Thus in a federal system one must seek the units of local

1

government below the level of the individual states. In the USA the federal system basically involves independent states which have relinquished certain powers, *e.g.* defence, to the federal government whilst retaining power over a wide range of governmental functions (subject to considerable judicial control). Thus in the USA it is the divisions of states which constitute the units of local government and not the States themselves.

In a unitary system the units of local government will be found directly below the level of the national government; *e.g.* in England and Wales the local government units have no intermediate level between themselves and the central government.

4. Classification by functions. Attempts have been made to classify local government according to the type of function which local authorities perform, and those which are performed by the central government. Under modern conditions of government such a classification has proved impossible, except in extreme cases; for instance no one would deny that defence is a central government function. Modern government involves the administration of many "national" services at a local level, and in allocating such services it is impossible to differentiate adequately on a logical basis, as opposed to one of convenience, between functions which are to be properly regarded as the domain of either the central or of the local authorities.

> NOTE: What may be popularly considered to be a "local" function must be considered in the light of its ramifications in the sphere of national economic and social policy; *e.g.* the effects of local authority housing programmes can only be considered in the light of national politics and its national economic and social effects.

5. Self-government. The term "local self-government" has been traditionally used of local government in England and Wales (and in Germany), and may be considered to be a principal feature of the English local government system (though by no means existing only in this country).

"The *Gemeinden* (local authorities) must be safeguarded in their right to regulate, under their own responsibility, all the affairs of the local community within the limit of the law"

(*Constitution of the Federal German Republic*). This illustrates the attitude towards local government which removes it from consisting of purely dependent organs of the state into an independent elected existence. The electoral basis of the system can be taken as the main distinction between the administration of local affairs by local government, and by the central government using local organs.

6. Local self-government in England and Wales. Local government units in England and Wales, though primarily units of local self-government, are at the same time units with local duties acting as ordered by the central government. One must not regard them as having complete independence, as this would be to deny the real power of the central government in the local field. They may however be compared with the local units in the USSR which are described in the constitution as "local organs of state power" (*see* VII), and are thus an example of local government as opposed to local self-government.

7. Classification by nature of function. It is not possible to define local government by reference to any one of the generally accepted divisions of government into legislative, executive, or judicial. Local government properly involves application of all these functions, and to define by reference to them would also cover by definition non-local government bodies, *e.g. regional hospital boards*.

NOTE: The growing tendency is to regard local authorities as mere executive (or administrative) outlets of the central government. This must not be allowed to disguise their legislative and judicial or quasi-judicial functions. The term " administrative" in the above sense, when applied to local authorities, must be considered as covering their political as well as their functional status.

FEATURES OF LOCAL GOVERNMENT

8. Basic features. It is possible at this stage to discern the following basic features of local government:

(a) *A subordinate system.* Local government implies a system of government which is subordinate to the central government, although not acting merely as a departmental agent of the central government, *e.g.* local offices of a ministry. It will be seen however that local government is not a self-sufficient entity and derives its power from the central government and its authority from the electors, and is substantially controlled and influenced by these facts.

(*b*) *Local scale.* It involves the administration of functions on a local scale, even though such functions may be properly classified as national in character, *e.g.* education.

(*c*) *Elected.* It involves in many states, including England and Wales, administration within the area of the local unit by elected persons, as opposed to administration by servants of the central authority.

(*d*) *Community services.* It is essentially a method of getting services run for the benefit of the community without any clear distinction between national and local affairs.

9. Basic distinctions. Local government represents the generally accepted fact of political life that all the functions of government cannot be run on the basis of central administration alone. It represents a mixture of central convenience and an admission that the centre is not omnipotent. Some measure of delegation being necessary, it is the form which such delegation takes which shows the basic distinction between local government and local *self*-government. Basically the central authority may choose to delegate on either of the following bases (but in fact its choice of methods of dispersal will involve a mixture of the two):

(*a*) *Devolution.* This involves the "farming out" of duties to local bodies as representatives of the central government, but without giving such bodies any autonomy. In this sense the local bodies are mere agencies of convenience of the central government and are formed and operated by it. They are merely "local organs of state power."

(*b*) *Decentralisation.* This involves the administration of functions by local bodies on the basis of local self-government.

NOTE: In England and Wales a mixture of decentralisation and devolution exists, with powers being allocated to local authorities and to direct localised outlets of state power. Despite the disappearance in the nineteenth century of the inherent right to local self-government, English local government may be regarded as true local self-government, and the local offices of the central administrative bodies are to be regarded as outside the system.

CHARACTERISTICS OF THE ENGLISH SYSTEM

10. Its subordinate nature. Local authorities are subordinate corporations formed by statute or by royal charter. The term *local authority* in England and Wales refers to a local government unit whose powers are vested in a council, elected by, and politically responsible to, a local electorate; but which is legally and administratively subordinate to, and created by, the central government.

NOTE: Despite this close central and local link, it is incorrect to classify local authorities as mere agents of that administration, as they retain organisational independence and a certain amount of policy-making power.

11. No Ministry of the Interior. There is no one central government department responsible for the overall supervision or control of local authorities. Although the Ministry of Housing and Local Government is concerned with a large area of local authority work, it is given no complete power of control. There is no body in England with powers comparable to that of a Minister of the Interior in certain foreign systems.

12. Obligatory functions. Although an authority may be given a discretion as to the way it chooses to act in certain cases, as a general rule local authorities are subject to many obligatory duties. In addition a local authority has no general power to act, and may only do so within the framework of powers legally conferred upon it.

NOTE: English local government law does not contain a "general competence" clause similar to that possessed by certain foreign systems, which would permit a local authority to carry out any acts which it considers advantageous to its area.

13. Degree of independence. The authorities have a degree of independence from the central government, particularly in such matters as the election of members; the appointment of staff; the introduction and mode of operation of certain services; and internal organisation. But apart from these matters local independence depends more upon local initiative than upon any inherent political or legal powers.

14. Absence of hierarchy. Although it may appear at first sight that certain authorities have a higher status than others, this must not be taken to indicate that a chain of control exists between the authorities. The feature of the English system is that authorities are basically functionally independent of each other, and there is no question of one authority being responsible or answerable to another. Differences exist because of status and not because of powers of control.

15. Elective basis. Council members are popularly elected and no council members are appointed by the government. Nor are there government officials responsible in each area for the performance of local authorities such as exist in France.

NOTE: Despite the general elective principle certain exceptions exist: co-option of persons to serve on committees (*see* VI, **19–21**), and the aldermanic system (*see* V, **7–11**). These exceptions however do not detract from the general elective principle, as control is retained by the elected members, although examples exist of the abuse of the aldermanic system.

16. Revenue. Local authorities have an independent source of revenue in *rates*. However, in recent years they have become increasingly dependent on the central government for finance, both directly through the grant system, and indirectly through the need to obtain consent to loans.

NOTE: Even though rates provide an independent source of revenue, the authority may only spend them on matters for which it has statutory authority.

17. Absence of sovereignty. Local authorities are not local parliaments. They do not possess sovereign legislative power and all their acts must be justified by law, or individual members may be exposed to financial penalties.

18. Functional allocation. In principal there is a correlation between the range of function and the type of local authority, each category of authority having a distinct set of powers. As a general rule the allocation of powers to a local authority is not based upon a consideration of the ability of the authority efficiently to exercise the powers. As will be seen, this represents a basic weakness in the English system of local government.

AD HOC AND MULTI-PURPOSE AUTHORITIES

19. Multi-purpose authorities. A characteristic of the modern system of local government in England and Wales is that local authorities administer a *range* of functions. The idea of *ad hoc* authorities administering a single function or group of functions which predominated during the nineteenth century has been rejected by the modern English system, and no longer exists on an elective basis. However, certain bodies administering individual aspects of what was previously the domain of local government still exist: *e.g.* Regional Hospital Boards; River Boards; Port Authorities; and certain joint boards.

20. Advantages of ad hoc (or special purpose) authorities. The following advantages of the special authority system may be noted, and it should be observed that special purpose authorities are widely used in American local government, particularly the school boards:

(*a*) *Urgency.* They may be set up with comparative ease to meet urgent administrative needs, and are consequently more flexible administrative tools than are local authorities.

(*b*) *Agreement on constituting.* Owing to their small size and less formalised nature, and to their limitation of purpose, agreement is more easily reached on the setting up of such authorities.

(*c*) *Representation of interests.* Owing to their non-elective basis it is possible to provide in their constitution for the representation of all interests affected.

(*d*) *Greater areas.* They may be set up where existing local authorities are too small in population or area to meet the needs of a particular service. By covering a wider geographical and a larger population catchment area than that which is provided by local authorities, they are able to remedy this basic weakness in providing efficient local government; *e.g.* the Metropolitan Police Authority and the Metropolitan Water Board.

(*e*) *Non-political.* Such boards may avoid the political divisions and disharmony which affect many elected local authorities.

21. Disadvantages of ad hoc authorities.

(*a*) *Over-utilisation of the system.* If there are too many special purpose authorities, this will lead to a repetition of the great nineteenth-century shortcoming of local authorities described as "a chaos of areas and a chaos of authorities."

(*b*) *Electoral chaos.* If the special authorities are to be constituted on an elected basis, this will result in a confusing multiplicity of elections, with a consequent decrease in interest in local elections (extremely low in any case), and a mere duplication of political representation.

(*c*) *Remoteness.* Multiplicity of authorities, and the possibility of fine functional divisions being drawn, will make it difficult for the public to know to whom to turn.

22. Advantages of multi-purpose authorities.

(*a*) *Less artificial divisions.* Services which are basically connected may be artificially divided between *ad hoc* authorities, with overlapping and wastage of resources. In the case of a multi-purpose authority this may be avoided by the council having an oversight of all departments, and providing a focal point for the public to consult.

(*b*) *Allocation of resources.* An important problem in any form of administration is the allocation of resources. There is thus the need for a body to be concerned with the general oversight of finance in order to consider and balance competing claims between the various services. It is felt that this is more easily achieved where a number of services are administered by one overall authority.

(*c*) *Knowledgeable membership.* The administration of a large number of functions by one authority enables its members to develop expertise in more than one aspect of the work, and thus to appreciate the competing demands of different services.

THE CONTINUANCE OF LOCAL SELF-GOVERNMENT

23. Present trend. The changed attitudes of the public and the government towards local government and the development of the welfare state have contributed to a weakening of the role of the local authority. In particular the central government has assumed the role of guardian of the interests of the citizens, and has adopted more and more powers to guide, stimulate and control local authorities. Local affairs and politics have become increasingly of marginal importance compared with national affairs, and what were traditionally local functions have fallen more and more into the national field.

24. Justification of state power. The following reasons may be advanced to support the view that local self-government is inappropriate at the present day in the light of the ever-increasing power of the central administration.

(a) *Communications.* The speed of communications at the present day as compared with the nineteenth century has greatly reduced time delays in administration. In consequence one justification of local government, its ability to deal with problems at a greater speed because of its nearness to the problem, has been reduced.

(b) *Planned economy.* The demands of a planned economy involve an ever-increasing concentration of power at the centre. Such power is not limited solely to economic decision-making but covers a wide range of social, transport and financial matters. Local authorities are too "local" to be viable units in a planned economy on a participation basis, and this presupposes that local government must become adapted to the requirements of a planned economy or suffer further reduction in powers.

(c) *Social welfare.* The national political parties have both supported a uniform social welfare programme, the achievement of which involves the growth of central control.

(d) *National minima.* It is becoming an accepted social and political fact of modern life that variations in the standard of services between varying areas is not to be tolerated. The development of local government in England and Wales has been on such a basis that wide variations in resources and in need exist between areas. This inadequacy has led to the development of a central grant system based on equalising resources and achieving national minimum standards. The growth of the financial role of the central authority has as a corollary reduced the power of the local units.

(e) *Structural defects.* The existing structure is a product of the nineteenth century, and its areas and allocation of functions is unrelated to the needs of the present day.

25. Arguments for the continuance of local government. It is suggested that, despite its considerable defects and its inability to compete with the central government, local government, or at least some form of it, may be desirable for the following reasons (these are developed more fully in XII):

(a) *Local variations.* Local authorities will acquire a greater knowledge of local variations and problems than is possible for the central authority. It is a fact of economic and social administration that actual needs can more adequately be evaluated by supervision at *ground level.*

(b) *Local interest.* Local interest and co-operation will through its intensity outweigh the possible advantages of efficiency which may be achieved through the transference of powers.

(c) *Impact.* Small areas make for easier and more effective impact of the citizen-consumer and official-producer relationship.

(d) *Political education.* Local authorities provide accessible areas of political education (an advantage considered favourably by both parties).

(e) *Correction of abuses.* The relative accessibility to the electorate and the sustaining of local interest by the council may provide a protection against the abuse by the central authority of its powers. Associations of local authorities may provide powerful "pressure groups" and have the influence to require consultation where local interests are affected.

PROGRESS TEST 1

1. What are the basic features of local government? (**1, 2, 8**)

2. What is the distinction between local government and local self-government? (**2, 5, 9**)

3. (a) How may the central government deal with administration at a local level? (**9**)

(b) At what level is local government located in federal and in unitary states? (**3**)

4. Can local government be defined in terms of:

(a) Nature of functions it administers? (**4**)

(b) Classification of functions? (**7**)

5. What are the general characteristics of the English system? (**10–18**)

6. Do you consider that local government should be administered by general or by special purpose authorities? (**19–22**)

7. Do you consider that power should be vested in the state or dispersed at a local level? (**23–25**)

CHAPTER II

THE HISTORY OF LOCAL GOVERNMENT

INTRODUCTION

1. Modern English local government. The modern English local government system is a product of the structural reforms and innovations of the nineteenth century caused by certain basic forces:

(a) *Machinery and urbanisation.* The mid-nineteenth century saw the culmination of the first great phase of urbanisation in English history caused by the development of machinery and the factory system of production, and the comparative reduction of dependence on agricultural production. The existing system proved inadequate to meet the needs of the new urban areas.

(b) *Political reform.* The extension of the franchise on a progressive basis led to the demand for participation and representation in local affairs, which had previously been denied to a large proportion of the newly enfranchised classes.

(c) *Functions of government.* The prevailing government attitude of *laissez-faire* gave way as the latter part of the century was reached, and the government adopted a different set of values as to its social obligations to the community.

2. Relevance of the history of local government. There was never a clean sweep of ideas and institutions dating from before the industrial revolution. Thus the ideas which, from 1832 onwards, were shaping modern local government, were tried at first within the framework of the then existing system. As a consequence there is a need to study the historical development of local government, as it is impossible to approach the structure of such a deeply-rooted system merely from the legal angle. It is necessary to examine the interaction of economic political, social, idealistic and legal factors which culminated in the development of the present institutions and the concepts which underly it, *e.g.* democratic control.

11

THE EARLY MEDIEVAL SYSTEM

3. Position up to 1327. The nature of local government during this earliest period is closely associated with the nature of central government.

The social and economic conditions prevailing during this period involved little communication; little labour mobility; little or no industry; and mainly a system of agricultural self-sufficiency. Governmental functions thus assumed a different emphasis from those of the present, and consisted mainly of the maintenance of internal order, and the regulation of local agriculture. In consequence local government areas reflected these objectives rather than an attempt to provide a nation-wide functional service as at present.

4. Local divisions. These varied considerably under the late Anglo-Saxon kings, but the Normans found a pattern of sorts which they regularised in their usual methodical way, as follows:

    (a) The country was divided into *shires* (or counties), which had been led by an earl under the Anglo-Saxons. (The first shires seem to have been formed by Alfred the Great, around centres to resist the Danes.)

    (b) The shires were divided into *hundreds*, which were governed by the hundred court, dealing with legal and administrative matters.

    (c) The hundred was divided into *vills* or townships, and each was represented in the hundred court by its reeve and four men, who answered for their fellows.

    (d) Some vills contained more than one parish, which was the area grouped round each church.

    (e) A few townships were outside the county system, as they had obtained privileges from the King, either by payment or by rendering a service to the Crown. So they had a measure of self-government, which usually included the right to hold a market and a court of their own.

5. The sheriff. William I used the sheriff as the key figure in local government and exerted royal control and influence through him. The office was a direct appointment from the King and care was taken to check the sheriff's authority to avoid the development of independent local power.

(a) *The functions of the sheriff.* These reflect the functions (or *lack of functions*) of local government during this period. They were principally concerned with presiding at the *county court*; commanding the *posse comitatus*, *i.e.* the full power of the county called out in the service of the King; charge of the *King's property*; accounting to the King for *county revenue*; providing a limited *police system*; and summoning and selecting the lesser barons for attendance at the nascent Parliament.

(b) *The development of the office.* It had a growing tendency to become oppressive, and after 1170 (*Inquest of Sheriffs*) it gradually declined until replaced for other than social purposes by the office of justice of the peace.

THE JUSTICES OF THE PEACE

6. Organisation. The office was mainly developed by Edward II to provide a system which was a compromise between the Norman centralising ideal and the Anglo-Saxon provincialism.

The direct responsibility of the sheriff gave way to the justice of the peace appointed to carry out certain state functions and to "keep the peace." The office dates from the reign of Edward I (1272–1307), but by 1327 the appointment was taken from the shire court and became exclusively a royal appointment.

7. Growth of the office. The social and economic disturbance of the Black Death and the consequent upheavals of the period accentuated the importance of the justice. In addition to the Black Death certain other factors combined to increase its authority:

(a) The growth of an itinerant labouring class.

(b) The growth of an embryo woollen industry under Edward IV which had achieved the status of a minor industry by the time of the Tudors.

(c) The problem of vagrancy, accentuated by the dissolution of the monasteries, which was tackled by the *Poor Law Act*, 1601.

8. Relations with local communities. By means of co-operation with local communities which displayed elements of local self-government (or at least local *self-help*) and by a gradual usurping of the administrative functions of the local courts, the justices acquired responsibility for local administrative duties. Eventually all such duties were exercised by the justices, and the importance of the office was enhanced by legislation imposing duties upon local authorities, *e.g.* the *Statute of Bridges*, 1530–1531; the *Highways Acts*, 1555 and 1562; and the *Poor Law Act*, 1601.

These functions were exercised by the justices in co-operation with local *parishes*.

PARISH GOVERNMENT

9. General situation. By 1832 there were in existence over 15,000 parishes, each being a distinct unit of local government, though never at any stage subjected to systematic treatment regarding constitution, areas, or function. The parishes were served by certain compulsory officers acting in conjunction with the justices, *viz.* the Constable, the Churchwarden, the Surveyor of Highways, and the Overseer of the Poor.

10. Legal basis of parish government. Two principal features, representing the prevailing attitude towards local government at the period, dominated the legal position of the parishes:

(*a*) *The right* of all inhabitants to participate in the administration of parochial business.

(*b*) *The duty* of all inhabitants to perform the duties of the various parochial offices.

11. The nature of parish government. This generally resolved itself into one of two forms:

(*a*) *The Open Vestry.* This form of government was open to the participation of all the inhabitants of the parish, was responsible for parish duties, and had the right to impose taxation on the inhabitants of the parish to provide finance for the carrying out of the duties.

(*b*) *The Select Vestry.* Generally the democratic form of the Open Vestry tended to concentrate the power of the parish in the hands of a limited number of inhabitants, either on a *de facto* or a *de jure* basis. The Select Vestry predominated in the City of London, Westminster, Bristol and in the Northern counties. The constitution was usually based on local custom, or established by local Act of Parliament. It generally consisted of between 12 and 24 parishioners either serving for life and filling vacancies by co-option, or some other form of entrenched power concentrated in the hands of a local oligarchy.

Although the Select Vestry could provide workable local government in a limited sphere, the tendency was towards lack of efficiency, degeneration and corruption.

12. The period 1800–1831. The traditional parish government was swallowed up by the rapidly growing population of the new industrial towns. The parish offices became an object of hatred and avoidance owing to their burdensome nature. Parliament had tended to use the parish as the administrative unit for new services, despite its inadequacy for the task, and consequently parish government became an anachronism in the fast-developing and changing society. Its adequacy for the limited tasks of the sixteenth and seventeenth century failed in the new conditions.

13. Reforming legislation. In certain limited cases examples of effective local government had emenated from the parishes, *e.g.* Woolwich and Liverpool. In these cases there was effective local democracy, the use of standing committees, and the employment of competent and qualified staff. These were however isolated examples, and steps were taken to attempt to remedy the situation.

The *Sturge Bourne Acts*, 1818–1819, made an effort to extend effective democracy to the parishes, but as the Acts required local adoption their permissive nature contributed to their almost total ineffectiveness. Similarly the *Hobhouse Act*, 1831, aimed at creating representative bodies in London responsible for all local government functions was unsuccessful (once again an adoptive Act).

THE BOROUGHS

14. Origin. These developed, particularly during the Tudor and Stuart periods, by the granting of royal charters to certain ancient townships which took them outside the general local government pattern. In many cases the charters were granted for the purpose of securing support in the developing Parliament, or in return for loans to the King. During the sixteenth century there was a tendency for such charters to hand over control to a select body, thus ending the participation of the general body of burgesses. The charters also granted to this

select body the right to make bye-laws and vested the municipal property in them.

15. Adequacy. In the sixteenth century the boroughs ran
their small areas in a reasonably efficient manner. They basically existed to protect the specific interest of traders and crafts-
men, and as such were adequate. However their inadequacies
were exposed with the demands placed upon them in the latter
part of the eighteenth century. They were unable to cope
with the problems of urbanisation and a growing population
requiring sanitary and building control. In addition their non-
democratic status led in many cases to inefficiency and corruption. (Note that three-quarters of the chartered boroughs were
governed by a closed body.)

THE IMPOTENCY OF THE JUSTICES

16. The urban age. The justices of the peace proved inadequate to cope with the problems attendant on the development
of urbanisation. They had neither the time nor the technical
skill and administrative ability to govern large urban areas and
provide public health and housing facilities.

Their powers had steadily grown since their creation in the
fourteenth century and covered such diverse matters as law
and order, the Poor Law, highways, bridges, paving, lighting
and cleansing, as well as a host of miscellaneous functions.
"Such an infinite variety of business had been heaped upon
them that few came to undertake, and fewer to understand,
the office" (*Blackstone*).

Also at this time forces were in motion that were to lead to
the realisation of the need to transfer the burden of the management of town and country away from persons of rank, and into
the hands of elected representatives and paid officials.

17. Position in 1832. In 1832 there existed 5,000 justices of
the peace, a number which, in relation to its past numbers, had
to deal with an increased number of functions, and proved
inadequate to cope with the increased demands of the office.
In many cases the office fell into the hands of "trading justices" concerned with providing some local services on a
profit-making basis.

18. An inadequate system. By the opening of the nineteenth century it had become clear that the old system was breaking down.

(*a*) County and parish could not cope with the problem of managing the new industrial towns.

(*b*) The other form of local government, namely the chartered borough, was unable to meet the needs of its own area, without considering many of the new areas with a need for strong and effective local government.

A situation was thus reached where a large number of new industrial centres, with the attendant public health, highways and health problems, were dependent on the hopelessly inadequate form of government provided by the justices of the peace.

NOTE: In the period 1689 to 1832 a large number of statutory authorities for special purposes were set up to deal with the urgent problems of the changing economic and social order: *e.g.* Guardians of the Poor; Turnpike Trusts; Improvement Commissioners responsible for paving, lighting and cleansing. Certain attempts had been made to create unions of such bodies, but only on a piecemeal basis. These *ad hoc* bodies did prove beneficial in some cases, but led to multiplicity of areas, and a confusion and overlapping of functions, and did not generally have sufficient powers to prove effective.

1832 TO 1888

19. Introduction. By 1832 the borough and county system had been swamped and was in ruins. The structure and the powers of the modern form of the old system were developed basically during this period through the following factors:

(*a*) *The interplay* of the revolutions in industry and science.
(*b*) The growth of *political democracy.*
(*c*) The *interaction* between the opposing concepts of centralisation and autonomous decentralisation.

NOTE: The nineteenth century belies the oft-quoted justification of local government that it is in the basis of democracy. In each case during the nineteenth century local government reforms followed the extension of the national franchise and were not causes of it (although the final extension of the franchise came after the municipal reform period).

20. Extension of the right to vote. The most important structural changes in local government during the nineteenth century followed, and can be largely attributed to, the extension of the franchise by the *Reform Acts* of 1832, 1867 and 1884.

(a) *The Reform Act*, 1832. This was followed in the first reforming phase by the *Poor Law Amendment Act*, 1834, and the *Municipal Corporations Act*, 1835.

(b) *The Reform Act*, 1867. This added to the middle classes, who were enfranchised by the 1832 Act, the urban artisans. It was followed by the establishment of the Local Government Board, 1871, and subsequently the Urban and Rural Sanitary Areas.

(c) *The Reform Act*, 1884. County Councils were established in 1888, following the enfranchisement of the agricultural labourers by the *Reform Act*, 1884.

21. Root causes of reform. Behind the Reform Acts themselves were the driving forces of the industrial, transport, medicine and engineering revolutions, the development in the techniques of taxation and the growth of political consciousness. These factors combined made it impossible for any government to disown responsibility for the essential elements of social security.

22. Local government in towns. The franchise of the eighteenth century was most corrupt in the towns. Therefore following the enfranchisement of the middle classes by the *Reform Act*, 1832, a demand arose for the reform of town government. The newly-enfranchised middle class pushed home the demand for reform of the towns, which limited participation to freemen and formed centres of privilege, indifference and political manipulation.

23. The Royal Commission of 1833. This was set up to study the state of the municipalities and "to collect information regarding the defects in the corporations and into elections and management of revenue etc." Its report unfairly tended to attribute general corruption to the boroughs, but made the main point that the private property rights of the old corporations should be taken for public use under the control of an elected assembly (though not a truly democratically elected one).

24. The Municipal Corporations Act, 1835. This Act outlined the form of government to apply to boroughs, and is still the basis of local government at the present day:

(a) A municipal corporation was defined as a "legal personification of the local community, represented by an elected council, and acting for, and responsible to, the inhabitants of the district."

(b) *The vote* was to be given to all rate-payers who had resided in the area of the corporation for a term of three years.

(c) *Council meetings* were to be open to the public.

(d) *An annual audit* of accounts was provided for.

(e) The administration of justice was separated from local administration.

(f) Provision was made for other urban areas to receive *a charter*.

(g) Provision was made for *the levying of a rate*.

(h) *A "borough fund"* was established.

25. Defects of the Act. Although the Act was a hitherto unheard-of confiscation of property rights of the old chartered corporations, it suffered from several notable defects.

(a) *Limited application.* The system did not apply to all urban areas; 246 bodies had municipal powers but only 178 were subject to the Act. London was regarded as too large and important to be subject to the Act, and 67 corporations were considered too insignificant.

(b) *No new system.* The Act did not provide a new structural system, and outside the municipal areas recourse still had to be had to non-elected justices and to a multitude of *ad hoc* authorities. There was thus left a "chaos of areas and a chaos of authorities"; this still prevails at the present day.

(c) *Powers.* The sphere of the new councils was extremely limited, and a need still remained for parliamentary or private legislation to extend the scope of the functions.

(d) *Areas.* No attempt was made to require the possession of a minimum area or minimum population essential to the proper and efficient exercise of municipal powers. (There was no "unionising" as under the Poor Law.)

(e) *Central control.* The principle of central government control was barely present with the exception of a form of audit without clear responsibility. Treasury sanction for loans, and the power to disallow bye-laws.

26. Extension of municipal powers. The powers of the boroughs were gradually extended by subsequent Acts of Parliament, and in 1872 the corporations became public health

authorities. By 1882 they had powers covering the regulation
of roads and streets; drainage and sewage; public health;
hospitals; gas and water supply.

In addition most of the larger boroughs had acquired special
powers as a result of their own initiative: *e.g.* Liverpool had
acquired a special *Sanitary Act* in 1846 and in 1867 Manchester
acquired an *Improvement Act* enabling it to deal with unfit
houses. Also by 1876, 62 new boroughs had been created, and
by 1882 a further 25.

27. Development of the public health movement. By 1851
half the population of England and Wales lived in towns; a
proportion which by 1881 had swelled to two-thirds. The early
pioneering work carried out by Chadwick as secretary to the
Poor Law Commissioners revealed the tremendous defects in
the urban environment, and in reports in 1838, 1842 and 1845
urged the enlarging of areas and authorities and the grant of
powers necessary for the effective handling of the problem.
The *Public Health Act*, 1848, set up the General Health Board
and local boards in areas with high death rates; 670 of these
local boards were established and designated as urban and
rural sanitary authorities.

The *Reform Act*, 1867, led to the setting up of the *Royal
Sanitary Commission* in 1868. Its report in 1871 revealed that
sanitary accommodation was extremely backward in the urban
areas and almost non-existent in rural areas. The report
recommended the establishment of strong and competent local
and central authorities. The role of the central authority was
assumed by the *Local Government Board* established in 1871,
and the role of the local authorities was assumed by the Urban
and Rural Sanitary Authorities established on a simplified
pattern by the *Public Health Act*, 1875.

28. Position up to 1888. For functions other than the
administration of the poor law and sanitation there were no
generally elected authorities outside of the boroughs. After
1871 education was administered by the School Boards. Thus
prior to the setting up of the rural and urban sanitary authorities large areas of each county were devoid of any really
effective unit of local self-government.

1888 to 1948

29. The Local Government Act, 1888. The Act applied the system of local self-government operating in the boroughs to rural local government. The principal features of the Act were:

(a) *Transfer of powers.* All the administrative powers of the justices of the peace in Quarter Sessions were transferred to elected county councils with the exception of control of the police. Members of the county councils were to be directly elected.

(b) *Geographical divisions.* Generally the new county structure followed that of the historical geographical boundaries, with a county council for each area. Special cases were Yorkshire with its three Ridings, and Lincolnshire with its three parks, and also Suffolk, Sussex, Cambridgeshire, and Northamptonshire each with two divisions.

(c) *London.* A new London County cut from three geographical counties was created.

(d) *Boroughs.* The largest boroughs, with populations of approximately 150,000, were excluded from the county structure. These were designated as county boroughs and became multi-purpose authorities exercising all functions of local government within their area independently of the county structure. The establishment of county boroughs caused considerable dispute among the older boroughs with smaller populations who feared a loss of power and status. Consequently the Act also excluded from the counties 57 municipal boroughs with populations of over 50,000, and four others of even lower populations, and designated these county boroughs.

NOTE: The Act may be criticised in that by inaugurating the system of county boroughs it deprived the county of a considerable slice of its rateable resources and set up a duality of structure. In addition general factors of population, resources and areas were not considered in setting up the administrative counties. Also the granting of county borough status to towns of less than 150,000 created authorities incapable of meeting efficiently the developing needs of local government.

30. The Local Government Act, 1894. The process of the establishment and democratisation of local government was completed by the Act of 1894. The Act extended a representative system (in fact the most democratic as no provision was made for aldermen) to newly created urban and rural district

B

councils. The former were areas of Improvement Act districts or Local Board districts under the Public Health Acts. The latter were parts of Unions not in a borough, Improvement or Local Board district. They obtained the powers of rural sanitary districts and Highways Boards.

In addition rural districts were subdivided into areas of parish councils and parish meetings. The former applied in parishes with a population exceeding 300. In parishes of populations between 100 and 300 a parish council could be constituted with permission of the county council. In parishes of under 100 the appropriate authority was the parish meeting.

31. Conclusions on the nineteenth century. The reforms of the nineteenth century, while establishing the principal component parts of the present system, suffered from considerable structural weaknesses.

(a) The *areas* chosen as local government areas were too small, their choice being occasioned mainly by geographical and historical accident, rather than by any consideration of optimum sizes for efficiency and effective local self-government.

(b) The system was constructed on a *ad hoc* basis without regard to an overall pattern or underlying concept of what form an effective system should take.

(c) The schism between town and country was ingrained and developed, even though the changing economic and social circumstances were working in an opposite direction. Thus an artificial structure was evolved.

(d) There developed the obstinate conviction that local authorities are self-contained, self-sufficient communities.

The resultant picture was thus one of a theoretically logical organisation but a practically diverse and illogical system, further confused by the existence of a large number of *ad hoc* authorities.

32. Ad hoc authorities. Although prevalent in the middle of the nineteenth century, these had gradually become functionally absorbed by the new units of local government. Following the transference of education in 1902, the only remaining exception was the Poor Law administered by the Boards of Guardians.

The Royal Commission on the Poor Law (1905) had recommended a complete revision of the system of administration of the Poor Law, but it was not until the *Local Government Act,*

1929, that the Boards were abolished and their functions transferred to the county and county borough councils. (The Act also revised the system of finance—*see* chapter IX.)

33. The Chelmsford Committee. The report of this committee in 1930 led to a clarifying and consolidating of the mass of legislation affecting local government. The *Local Government Act*, 1933, the *Public Health Act*, 1936, and the *Food and Drugs Act*, 1938, greatly clarified the law and thus ensured by 1939 that there was "the beginning of a consistent code of local government law and a uniform hierarchy of local authorities" (*W. O. Hart*).

34. Functions. The twentieth century has seen an extension of the functions of local authorities, through an extension also involving the reallocation of functional responsibility between authorities, and between local authorities and the central government. Two particular developments may be discerned:

(*a*) The transference of functions from smaller to larger local authorities, *e.g.* education from the districts to the counties.

(*b*) Since the Second World War a transfer of functions from local authorities to either public boards of the nationalised industries, or to *ad hoc* boards. The feature of the *ad hoc* boards being their non-elective character, and the fact that they cover wider geographical areas and larger population catchment areas than those of local authorities, *e.g.*

(*i*) Hospital administration was transferred by the *National Health Service Act*, 1946, to Regional Hospital Boards and to Hospital Management Committees.

(*ii*) In 1936 responsibility for trunk roads was transferred to the Ministry of Transport.

(*iii*) Police functions were removed from districts to counties under the *Police Act*, 1946.

(*iv*) The *Fire Services Act*, 1947, and *Town and Country Planning Act*, 1947, transferred these functions to the counties.

(*v*) Gas and electricity were nationalised in 1947 and 1948 respectively, and their administration removed from local boards to nationalised public boards.

35. Functional gains. There has been an extension of powers of the larger local authorities, particularly under the *Town and Country Planning Act*, 1947, and the *Children Act*, 1948.

36. Structural reorganisation. The work of the Royal Commissions and the reforms, particularly the *London Government Act* are dealt with in XII (Reform) and IV (London Government).

CONCLUSIONS

37. Central control. The twentieth century has seen such a tremendous increase in central administrative control that the existence of local government as autonomous units is thought to be seriously in doubt (*see* XII).

38. Summing up. Despite the transfer of functions, the larger boroughs and districts have achieved some recompense through the technique of *delegation*. The *Education Act*, 1944, provides an example of the process of centralisation taking place, but with the recognition of the needs of the larger authorities which would otherwise be stripped of their powers. While centralising the administration of education at the county level, the Act provides that authorities with populations exceeding 60,000 could apply for the status of "excepted" districts, and thus achieve control of day-to-day administration. Smaller towns may also be grouped with rural districts to perform the more limited duties of divisional executives. The *Local Government Act*, 1958, added health and welfare services to the list of functions that could be delegated to boroughs and urban districts with populations of 60,000 or more.

PROGRESS TEST 2

1. Why was the modern English system of local government principally a product of the nineteenth century? (**1, 16, 18–21**)

2. Trace the development of local government down to 1832, (**3–15**) paying particular attention to the role of:
    (*a*) The sheriff. (**5**)
    (*b*) The justices. (**6–13**)
    (*c*) The boroughs. (**14, 15**).

3. Why was the pre-1832 system inadequate to meet the demands of the nineteenth century? (**14–19**)

4. Outline the nineteenth century local government reforms. (**20, 22–30**)

5. What was the significance of the Public Health movement to local government reform? (**27, 30**)

6. What principle changes have occurred in the twentieth century? (33–34)

7. What conclusions can be drawn from local government development in the nineteenth century? (31)

8. Outline the development of the boroughs in English local government. (14, 15, 22–26)

9. What role have *ad hoc* authorities played in the development of the English local government system? (18, 31, 32, 34)

CHAPTER III

THE STRUCTURE OF LOCAL GOVERN-MENT IN ENGLAND AND WALES

GENERAL FEATURES

1. Basic aspects. Before considering the structural defects of the English local government system, the following general aspects may be pertinently considered, as set out in **2–4** below.

2. Distribution of functions.

(*a*) *The tier system.* In any particular area functions will be administered by varying local government units. In urban areas local authority functions will be administered by the county council (*first-tier*), and by the urban district or borough council (*second-tier*). In rural areas a three-tier system operates, and functions will be administered by the county council, the rural district council (*second-tier*), and by the parish council or meeting (*third-tier*).

In Greater London the first-tier authority is the Greater London Council, and the second-tier the London boroughs.

The only non-tier authority is the county borough which exercises all the functions of local government within its area.

(*b*) *"All-purpose" authorities.* It follows from the above that the underlying distinction between the county borough and all other local authorities is that the former exercises all the functions of local government within its area, whereas in other cases there is a sharing of functional responsibility.

(*c*) *Absence of hierarchy.* English local government structure is not organised on a hierarchical structure. There is no pattern of smaller areas being responsible to and under the control of the larger authorities. Within its own sphere each local authority enjoys a functional independence: *i.e.* it is responsible for the administration of a group of services, or parts of services, and is not subordinated to another authority in the exercise of these powers.

(*d*) *Functional incoherence.* A feature of English local government has been the tendency to allocate a function to a *type* of local authority without considering whether particular local authorities, within that type, have the size or resources to administer the new service efficiently.

26

3. Historical divisions.

(a) *Lack of uniformity.* The development of local government in the nineteenth century and its establishment on its present basis was largely concerned with the adaptation of historical units to changing circumstances. Units were established primarily by the Anglo-Saxon and Danish rulers on a basis of military needs. As a consequence considerable variations in size of area, population and resources exist between local authorities of the same legal status.

(b) *Town and country.* English local government is firmly based on the separate existence and needs of urban and rural areas, despite the spread of the conurbations which have largely contributed to the lack of realism in this division at the present day. But note here the bringing of areas of countryside into borough areas in certain cases: *e.g.* Reading and Basingstoke.

(c) *Districts and boroughs.* With the exception of certain rather unimportant powers to make bye-laws the only difference between non-county boroughs and districts (particularly urban districts) is that of title and ceremony; and also the much criticised aldermanic principle (*see* V, **7–11**).

4. Other features.

(a) *Elections.* English local authorities are elected by periodic public elections by the citizens of the area represented.

(b) *Finance.* Local authorities are dependent to a large extent on local financial revenue, thus ensuring a closer responsibility to the electors of the area.

THE PRESENT STRUCTURE

5. Sources. The sources of the present structure of local government in England and Wales are found in the *Local Government Act*, 1933, and the *London Government Act*, 1963. *The 1933 Act* states that "for the purpose of local government England and Wales shall be divided into administrative Counties and County Boroughs. Administrative Counties shall be divided into County Districts; these being Non-County Boroughs, Urban and Rural Districts. County Boroughs and Rural Districts shall consist of one or more Parishes." Therefore outside London there are six basic local government units, plus the provision for the creation of rural boroughs contained in the *Local Government Act*, 1958.

The *London Government Act*, 1963, abolished the old London

County Council and the Counties of Middlesex and parts of Essex, Surrey and Kent, and replaced them with the Greater London Council and 32 London boroughs, whilst leaving unaffected the anachronistic Common Council of the City of London. (This is dealt with fully in IV.)

6. Joint boards and committees. In certain cases two or more local authorities may form a joint authority for the administration of a public service over a wider area for reasons of convenience and economy. Such authorities are not directly elected, and representatives are often appointed by the constituent councils. Finance is obtained from charges, contributions from constituent councils, or from the central government. *Alternatively* local authorities may delegate certain functions to a joint committee appointed by them. *Examples* of joint boards exist under the provisions of the *Public Health Act*, 1936; the *Water Act*, 1945; and the *Town and Country Planning Act*, 1962.

7. Special local authorities. In certain cases the government may set up special local authorities outside the usual structure to deal with particular local functions. Common examples of special authorities are those dealing with the management of harbours and docks; land drainage; protection and control of fisheries.

Members are sometimes appointed by local authorities, sometimes by the beneficiaries of the services, and sometimes by the central government. Though not directly elected it is usual for them to contain representatives of the general public interest and representatives of those directly affected.

8. Overlapping. In certain cases local functions are provided by public utilities: *e.g.* gas and electricity supply through local boards, and hospitals through regional boards. In addition facilities such as public transport may be provided by private enterprise. Thus the domain of local government merges into that of government ownership and that of private enterprise.

THE COUNTY

9. Nature. The typical *administrative county* (so called to distinguish it from the judicial and geographical areas which may not be co-terminous) is predominantly rural in character, but with substantial urban areas comprising the greater part of its population and financial resources. These urban areas are non-county boroughs and urban districts.

Administrative counties are substantially the same as geographical counties; but it must be remembered that the administrative county does not include the County Borough areas which are inside its perimeter, although they are part of the geographical county.

10. Establishment. They are established by the *Local Government Act*, 1888, which provided that for every administrative county there should be elected a county council, entrusted with the administrative and financial business of the county. Generally they are co-extensive with the geographical county, but in certain cases sub-divisions of a geographical county into two or more administrative counties have been made:

(a) *Lincolnshire.* Divided into Holland, Kesteven and Lindsey.

(b) *Suffolk.* Divided into East and West Suffolk.

(c) *Sussex.* Divided into East and West Sussex.

(d) *Yorkshire.* Divided into the East, West and North Ridings.

(e) *Hampshire.* Divided into Hampshire and the Isle of Wight.

NOTE: In 1965 the Soke of Peterborough was amalgamated with Huntingdonshire to form a single county and council, and the separate Isle of Ely County Council was amalgamated with Cambridgeshire. In 1963 the *London Government Act* abolished the counties of London and Middlesex.

11. Constitution. County councils consist of chairmen, aldermen and councillors (*see* V and VI).

12. Disparities. Wide disparities exist in the size of population, areas and financial resources between the counties, as follows:

(a) *Population.* Lancashire has a population in the region of 2½ million, whereas the population of Radnorshire is approximately 20,000.

(b) *Area.* The area administered by the Devonshire County

Council covers 2,583 square miles, whereas the Isle of Wight covers 147 square miles.

(c) *Resources.* The rateable value of Lancashire is £77 million, and that of Radnorshire £½ million.

13. Functions. The principal functions of a county council are education; health; fire and ambulance services; libraries; highways; town and country planning; supervision of housing in rural areas; laid drainage; child welfare services; and registration of births, death and marriage.

NOTE: County councils are not rating authorities, but raise their finance by precepts issued to districts within their administrative area.

COUNTY BOROUGHS

14. Nature. These are generally large urban areas exceeding a certain population figure, and either constituted by the *Local Government Act*, 1888, or subsequently. There are 82 at the present and they administer all the functions of local government within their areas.

NOTE: Certain county boroughs have the title of "city" but this is of no legal significance.

15. Creation. The original object of the 1888 Act was to confer county borough status only on authorities exceeding 50,000 in population. It however pandered to the demands of many of the older boroughs, and conferred the status upon them irrespective of their suitability to act as county boroughs and to meet the population figure. Consequently a large number of county boroughs exist which are indefensible within the present system, as they tend unjustifiably to break up the administrative uniformity of the county structure and to deprive the county of a large portion of its rateable value.

16. Disparities. In 1965, 35 county boroughs were in existence with populations of under 100,000. Wide variations exist in size, area and rateable resources. For instance, Birmingham has a population exceeding 1 million and covers an area of 80 square miles, whilst Canterbury has a population of 30,000 and an area of 7½ square miles. The discrepancies were especially noticeable before the *London Government Act*, as many boroughs and urban districts in the Greater London area had populations considerably larger than a high proportion of the county boroughs.

NON-COUNTY (OR MUNICIPAL) BOROUGHS

17. Constitution. These have the same constitution as a county borough: *i.e.* mayor, aldermen and councillors, but functionally they are identical to urban districts. Mostly they are ancient townships of particular rank and importance which have been granted a Royal Charter of incorporation at some time in their history.

18. Present pattern. At present there are 270 boroughs. Populations vary widely, and 20 have a population of under 2,500; 50 a population of under 5,000, and a further 36 a population between 5,000 and 10,000. Areas governed range from 5 to 13 square miles; resources from £14,000 to £7 million rateable value; and populations from 1,000 to 100,000 (before the *London Government Act* this figure exceeded 200,000).

19. Creation. They may be created by Order under the *Local Government Act*, 1958, or more commonly, under old Royal Charters.

20. Rural boroughs. The *Local Government Act*, 1958, makes provision for the creation of rural boroughs. These will be ancient non-county boroughs which because of their size are unable to fulfil adequately the functions of a borough. They will retain their ancient privileges but take on the functional status of a parish council.

DISTRICT COUNCILS

21. Establishment. Urban and rural districts are based upon the Urban and Rural Sanitary Districts created under the *Public Health Acts*, 1872 and 1874. They are established on their present basis by the *Local Government Act*, 1894.

22. Constitution and nature. They both have a chairman and councillors.

Urban districts are usually compact townships having larger populations than rural districts, but administering a much smaller area. *Rural districts* generally cover a large country area contiguous to a medium-sized rural township.

Populations vary, but half the urban districts have a population of under 20,000. The extreme variations in urban districts are:

(a) *Population.* The largest is Thurrock with 120,000, the smallest Llantwrytd Wells with 550.

(b) *Area.* Acreage governed varies from 122 acres to 49,000 acres.

(c) *Rateable value* varies from £13,000 to £7 million.

Rural districts are large areas with small populations, and four-fifths have a population of between 5,000 and 30,000. Acreage governed varies between 4,000 and 361,000; and rateable value between £22,000 and £4 million.

23. Functions. The principal functions of districts (including boroughs) include building control; public health; housing; highways; education in certain cases where the population exceeds 60,000; inspection of food and drugs; and the levying of rates.

PARISHES

24. Constitution and nature. Rural parishes with a population exceeding 300 must have a parish council consisting of a chairman and councillors. If the population is between 200 and 300 the county must create a parish council if requested by the parish to do so. If the population is under 200 a parish meeting will suffice, but a council may be created at the discretion of the county. Note that urban parishes have no legal significance.

Rural parishes are subdivisions of rural areas and generally small villages with low populations.

25. Functions. Typical functions of a parish council include management of allotments; swimming baths; burial grounds; administration of bye-laws; footpaths; litter prevention; suppression of nuisances; parks; lighting of roads.

TESTS OF STRUCTURE

26. General. As will be seen one of the principal grounds of criticism of local government, and the basis of reform proposals, is the structural weakness of the system.

The defects of the structure of local government are dealt with in XII, and at this stage it is merely proposed to consider certain criteria with which it is thought that an effective and efficient structure should comply.

27. Structural criteria.

(a) *The administrative context of local government.* To date, the guiding structural criteria have largely been adherence to historic divisions of counties and boroughs, and to the conferment of local authority status on geographically homogeneous areas.

As a result of this unmethodical approach, disparities in areas, populations and financial resources have resulted, and prevented the maximising of efficiency. Local pride has made it difficult to alter areas and status, and reforms have been largely on a minor basis.

(b) *Maximising of efficiency.* Local government structural units should be of such a size as to enable maximum efficiency and economy of service to be achieved. At present many areas are too small to reap the benefits of large-scale economies or to warrant the employment of highly qualified staff.

(c) *Democratic control.* In addition to mere overall efficiency and economy, an area should not be of too unwieldy a size to prevent effective control of officials by the elected representatives.

(d) *Responsiveness to local needs.* Local government, being concerned with the local effectiveness and operation of services, must not assume a character and size which causes it to lose contact with individual areas and become unresponsive to local needs.

Thus local government structure should ideally be at an optimum size which is able to reap the economies and other benefits of large-scale organisation, but yet not lose touch with the individuals and areas of any given structure.

ALTERATION IN AREA AND STATUS

28. Alteration in status.

(a) *Charters of incorporation.* An urban or rural district may present a petition to the Queen praying for elevation to the status of borough (*Local Government Act, 1963*).

Such a petition must come from a majority decision of the whole council, and be reaffirmed at least one month after the first resolution. The petition is referred to the Committee of the Privy Council, and will generally contain details supporting the application showing that the authority has adequate administration, equipment and distinct civic life sufficient to warrant the grant of borough status.

A local inquiry will be held and, in addition to examining the reasons given by the council, attention will be paid to the character of the district and the advantages and disadvantages of conferring borough status on the area. If the Committee is satisfied, a draft charter must be submitted by the council and a Bill of Confirmation will be passed.

(b) *County borough status.* A local authority may present a Private Bill to acquire county borough status, provided its population is over 100,000. Promotion may also be conferred by Order in Council subject to parliamentary approval.

In applications for promotion the prime qualification is the fitness of the local authority to discharge the functions of a county borough. For this the administrative record of the authority and its financial position will be considered. Also of considerable importance is the effect of promotion on the county of which the authority forms part, as the loss of a large urban area will greatly reduce the financial resources of the county, which will probably not be compensated by the lower expenditure occasioned.

29. Alteration in area.

(a) *Alterations under Local Government Act, 1958.* The review carried out by the Royal Commissions of 1958 and the review of districts by the counties is dealt with in XII, **20–25**.

(b) *County and county borough boundaries.* Both counties and county boroughs may make representations to the Minister of Housing and Local Government for the alteration of their own areas by change of boundary, by union or by division. The Minister is empowered, after holding a local inquiry, to make orders to confirm or vary the proposals. Such an order is subject to the approval of both Houses of Parliament.

(c) *County review. See* XII, **20**.

PROGRESS TEST 3

1. What are the basic features of the structure of local government in England and Wales? (2–4)

2. What *local* functions are dealt with outside the general structure? (5–8)

3. Outline the nature, constitution and functions of the administrative county, and give examples of disparities existing between areas. (9–13)

4. What are county boroughs? How may this status be achieved? (14–16, 28)

5. What is the constitution of municipal boroughs? Give examples of the present pattern of such authorities? (17–19)

6. What are rural boroughs? (20)

7. Outline the nature, constitution and functions of district councils. (21–23)

8. Outline the nature, constitution and functions of parish government. (24–25)

9. What tests should a suitable local government structure satisfy? (26, 27)

10. How may alterations in status and areas be achieved? (28, 29)

CHAPTER IV

LONDON GOVERNMENT

HISTORY

1. Position in 1835. By 1835 London had a population exceeding one million, and covered an area of 22 square miles. Government was the responsibility of 172 vestries and a large, irregular pattern of *ad hoc* authorities: *e.g.* paving, lighting and cleansing boards, police and highway authorities, sewer authorities, etc. A suggestion that the City Corporation should include surrounding suburbs was rejected.

2. Development in the 1850s. In 1854 a Royal Commission recommended the establishment of a body with responsibilities covering certain services over the whole area. As a result the *Metropolis Local Management Act*, 1855, created the *Metropolitan Board of Works* consisting of 45 members under a paid chairman. The members were not directly elected by the citizens, but by the larger vestries and the district boards representing groups of parishes. The Board had no powers in the area of the City of London but was responsible in the 117 square miles which had formerly been the area of the *Metropolitan Commissioner of Sewers*, for the provision of drainage, paving, lighting, cleansing and improvement of the area.

The *principal problem* facing the Board was that of providing an adequate sewage system to prevent pollution of the Thames. In addition they took over the provision of other services such as maintenance of river embankments; fire services; regulation of offensive trades; control of buildings as regards height and frontage lines. In the matter of control of buildings their area was divided into 67 sub-districts.

3. Defects of the Board. The Board, despite its fairly wide powers, suffered from the following defects:

(a) It was not directly elected by the citizens or ratepayers.

(b) There was a complete absence of any central government control and assistance.

(c) *Ad hoc authorities.* There co-existed major *ad hoc* authorities administering services that should have been dealt with by the Board; they added to the confusion of the system. An example was the *London Schools Board.*

(d) *Powers of enforcement.* The Board did not have sufficient powers to compel the various district boards and vestries to carry out their duties, or to maintain adequate standards of service in so doing.

4. Population developments. The improvement in transport in the 1860s led to the development of a suburban sprawl. The opportunities for employment in London also tended to attract a large number of working-class families to London, and their general poverty and frequent unemployment led to a great increase in tenement living and its attendant social problems.

In addition certain of the inner suburban areas had enormous population increases during the nineteenth century, and particularly during the latter half of the period: *e.g.* the population of West Ham increased from approximately 2,500 in 1801 to 267,000 in 1901, and was attended by the building of over 120 factories in the area during the century.

NOTE: The population of Inner London grew from 2·4 million in 1851 to 4·5 million in 1901; and the population of the outer suburbs from 0·3 million in 1851 to 2·0 million in 1901.

REFORMING LEGISLATION

5. Local Government Act, 1888. The Act created a new authority to replace the Metropolitan Board of Works by establishing the *London County Council* to govern *"central"* London. The old area of the MBW was thus transferred to the Administrative County of London which included the City of London in its area but left the ancient city government virtually untouched. The powers of the Board were increased in the hands of the LCC which consisted of 124 councillors and 20 aldermen. The Act however permitted certain *ad hoc* bodies to remain, *e.g.* the School Board and the Thames Conservancy Board; it also kept intact the old vestry and district board system.

The Act however was deficient in that it limited the increase in powers to such matters as the improvement of highways, the right to promote and oppose Bills, and the appointment of medical officers. The fear of extending the powers of the LCC, and of reducing the powers of the vestries and districts, was due basically to the fear that radical elements would dominate the LCC and would dominate the more local authorities.

6. London Government Act, 1899. The mass of vestries and districts was replaced in 1899 by 28 *metropolitan boroughs*. Thus a two-tier system was built up for London with the LCC principally responsible for housing (shared power), planning, education, welfare, parks, finance, child care, main drainage, fire services, etc. The metropolitan boroughs were responsible for housing, public health, rating, bye-laws, roads and highways and recreational facilities. Each borough had its own mayor, aldermen and councillors.

The Act was principally *defective* for the following reasons:

(*a*) *Compromise.* The fear of radicalism which had dominated the thinking behind the 1888 Act again dominated the 1899 Act, with the result that an overall system was not devised, but one aimed at the boroughs effectively counterbalancing the power of the LCC, with consequent wastage and loss of efficiency and co-operation.

(*b*) *Urban spread.* Population and travel developments soon resulted in the development of an extensive built-up area, effectively London, but spreading beyond the boundaries of the LCC, and administered by varying bodies such as the Middlesex County Council, urban districts and boroughs, and county boroughs such as East and West Ham and Croydon.

(*c*) *Dependence.* The system created by the Acts would not have worked had it not been for the continued existence of various *ad hoc* authorities covering a wide area: *e.g.* Police, Water, Port of London, Traffic and Licensing, Gas and Electricity Authorities.

GREATER LONDON

7. Twentieth century developments. The century has seen continued *outward* growth, with a steady population decline in the inner areas, particularly the City of London. This has been accelerated by slum clearance and rehousing in outer areas, office growth, improvement in travelling and the growth of the commuter class, building policies, and the effects of the Second World War.

No action followed the *Reading Committee* in 1945 or the

Clement Davis Committee in 1946 basically because of the impossibility of distinguishing between the problems of the LCC and those of greater London as a whole, and the need for a Royal Commission.

8. The Royal Commission on Local Government in the London Area, 1957.

(a) *Terms of reference.* The Commission under Sir Edwin Herbert was set up "to examine the present system and working of local government in the greater London area; to recommend whether any, and if so, what, changes in the local government structure and the distribution of local government functions in the area, would better secure effective and convenient local government."

(b) *Area.* The original area contemplated covered 842 square miles, but this was subsequently reduced by Parliament and by the Commission itself to 616 square miles. It covers a 15-mile radius from Charing Cross, and a population of just over 8 million.

9. The Herbert Report. The Report began by commenting on what it considered to be the two fundamental defects in the existing structure:

(a) *Wide basis.* There existed no body responsible for administering for the whole area those functions which required a metropolis-wide basis for efficient administration.

(b) *Functions.* There was a lack of relationship between areas and their functions, and in particular there existed a functional weakness in the districts, which the Commission viewed as the basic units of local government.

10. The Commission's remedies. To remedy these two principal defects, the Commission's recommendations for reform were as follows:

(a) *Greater London Council.* There should be a directly elected body set up responsible for the strategic aspects of planning and education, and for the administration of services which needed to be administered on an area-wide basis: *i.e.* overspill housing, main drainage, major highway and housing projects, urban redevelopment, refuse disposal, fire services and major open spaces.

NOTE: The GLC should only perform those functions for which there is a strong case for metropolis-wide administration, and the council should be directly elected with sufficient executive powers to enable it to control purely local interests.

(b) *Changes of structure*. The Commission recommended the abolition of the existing structure of counties, and the amalgamation of the existing boroughs and districts into London boroughs with populations between 100,000 and 250,000. These would carry out those functions not allocated to the GLC.

The Commission stressed the desirability of placing certain services closer to the public. In particular the boroughs should handle health and welfare services; planning control functions; and the day-to-day administration of education.

11. Government acceptance. The Government in its White Paper, *London Government. Government Proposals for Reform* (Cmnd. 1592, 1961) accepted in general the main proposals of the Commission, subject to two important exceptions:

(a) *Education*. The dividing up of education functions between the GLC and the London boroughs was rejected. Basically the Government favoured education being a borough responsibility, but because of the previous unified system of the LCC and the lack of experience of the old metropolitan boroughs, a compromise was accepted. By this the London boroughs outside the old LCC area became education authorities, whereas those inside became subject to the *ad hoc* arrangement of the Inner London Education Authority, with the position to be reviewed in 1970.

(b) *Size*. The Government enlarged the borough population criteria laid down in the Herbert Report to between 180,000 and 330,000.

Other departures from the Report consisted in the giving of various fringe areas the right to opt out of the general scheme, and the decision to transfer the functions of the Metropolitan Water Board to the GLC.

12. The London Government Act, 1963. Despite considerable opposition to the Act by the LCC, the parliamentary Labour Party and certain other interests such as the Middlesex County Council, the Act received the Royal Assent in July 1963. The *principal provisions* of the Act are:

(a) 32 London boroughs were created out of the existing authorities, and amalgamations ranging in size of population from Sutton with approximately 170,000 inhabitants to Lambeth with over 340,000.

(b) The administrative counties of London and Middlesex and the other previously existing authorities ceased to exist.

(c) The special status of the City of London was to continue, with the authorities having the same powers as a London borough.

(d) The area of the London boroughs and the City was to be administered for certain functions by the Greater London Council.

(e) The Inner London Education Authority was established to provide education services in the old LCC area.

(f) Parts of Essex, Hertfordshire, Kent and Surrey were taken into the GLC's area.

13. Constitutions.

(a) *The GLC.* This consists of 100 councillors and 16 aldermen, with each of the London boroughs being an electoral area and returning from two to four councillors depending on size of population.

For electoral purposes the cities of Westminster and London are to form one area. *Councillors* are elected for three years and retire *en masse*; and *aldermen* amounting to one-sixth of the councillors are indirectly elected for six years, with one-half retiring every three years.

(b) *The London boroughs.* Each has a mayor, deputy mayor, aldermen and councillors. Councillors serve for three years and retire together, and aldermen amounting to one-sixth of the councillors serve for six years, with half retiring every three years.

14. Functions.

(a) *Finance.* The boroughs are rating areas with the GLC a precepting authority. In place of the London Equalisation Scheme provision is made for payments on a formula basis by the GLC to the boroughs for the first eight years.

(b) *Housing.* Initially the GLC has wider powers than envisaged. In addition to the main rehousing responsibilities, it will administer the LCC's housing functions with eventual redistribution to the boroughs. Responsibility will then only be for major re-developments, etc.

(c) *Planning.* While the GLC retains overall control, the Act grants to the boroughs the right to formulate the borough development plan.

(d) *Education.* The ILEA in the old LCC area, and the London boroughs outside it.

15. Shared functions.

(a) *Highways.* Major highways (shared with the Ministry) are the responsibility of the GLC together with newly-designated metropolitan roads, while all other roads other than trunk roads are the responsibility of the boroughs.

(b) *Planning: see* **14**(c) above.

(c) *Housing: see* **14**(b) above.

(d) *Parks.*

(e) *Sewage and sewage disposal.* The boroughs control drains and sewers other than main sewers.

(f) *Building control.* The GLC has control, subject to designation in inner boroughs.

16. Other functions.

(a) *The boroughs.* Personal health services; maternity and child welfare, mental health; children; libraries; registration; sanitation; food and drugs; elections; refuse collection; inspection for health, etc.

(b) *The GLC.* Fire service; ambulance service; refuse disposal; licensing.

17. Importance of the London Government Act. The Act marks an important stage in the development and reform of local government for the following reasons:

(a) *Need for overall authority.* The Act recognises the need for a single authority covering a wide area and administering those functions which depend for effective administration on a large area and population catchment zone.

(b) *Retention of local units.* By retaining to a large extent, subject to amalgamations, the local units and strengthening their functions, the Act recognises the need for true local government to be *local*. The London boroughs represent a compromise between the efficiency and economy of size and the need to keep essentially personal services close to the users. Also, by substantially retaining local entities, personal identification with the authorities is maintained.

PROGRESS TEST 4

1. Outline the historical development of London government down to (but not including) the Act of 1963.   **(1–7)**

2. What was the function of the Herbert Commission? **(8)**

3. What principle recommendations did the Herbert Report contain? **(9–10)**

4. To what extent were its suggested remedies accepted by the Government? **(11)**

5. What were the main provisions of the *London Government Act*, 1963? **(12–16)**

6. What was the significance of the Act? **(17)**

CHAPTER V

THE PERSONNEL OF LOCAL AUTHORITIES

THE MEMBERS

1. Qualifications for membership. The law does not concern itself with the suitability of a candidate for membership of a local authority. This is the responsibility of the electors. The law does, however, make certain provisions to ensure that councillors have an interest in the affairs of the locality.

To be a member of a local authority a person must be of full age, and be a British citizen, and in addition he must satisfy at least *one* of the following requirements:

(*a*) He must be on the register of local government electors for the area.

(*b*) He must own freehold or leasehold land in the area of the authority.

(*c*) He must reside in the area during the whole of the twelve months preceding the election.

2. Disqualifications from membership. The law contains the following positive provisions about disqualification from membership:

(*a*) *Arising from employment.* A person is disqualified from membership of a local authority if he holds any paid office or other place of profit which is in the gift or disposal of the council or any of its committees: *e.g.* teachers or other persons employed in schools or educational institutions maintained or assisted by the council are ineligible for membership (but not from sitting on the education committee of a local authority).

(*b*) *Financial incapacity.* A person who is a bankrupt or who has entered into a composition with creditors is disqualified from membership of a local authority.

(*c*) *Imprisonment.* The commission of an offence within the five years previous to the election, involving imprisonment for three months or more (without the option of a fine) involves disqualification, irrespective of the nature of the offence.

(*d*) *Surcharge.* A person who has been surcharged for an

amount of over £500 is disqualified from council membership for a period of five years from the date of the surcharge.

(e) *Attendance*. Failure to attend council meetings without reasonable excuse for a period of six months will involve disqualification.

MAYORS AND CHAIRMEN

3. Formal appointment. The first business transacted at the first council meeting is the election of a mayor or chairman, whichever is appropriate in the particular authority.

The hierarchy of each council is headed by an *indirectly elected* mayor or chairman, offices which combine functional aspects with a considerable role of ceremonial nature.

NOTE: The right to appoint a *Lord Mayor* is granted to certain cities by Royal Letters Patent, but this special designation has no functional or legal significance.

4. Chairman. Authorities not presided over by a mayor will be presided over by a chairman who will undertake much the same functional and ceremonial role as the mayor. This applies to all authorities except county boroughs and boroughs. In the case of a county council the appointment of a vice-chairman is obligatory, but it is discretionary in district councils.

5. The office of mayor. He is elected by the council, and although he is usually a council member this is not obligatory, provided he has the qualifications to be a councillor and suffers from none of the disqualifications. He fulfils the role of *presiding member* of the council and is legally entitled to take the chair at all council meetings. His term of office is for one year. He has the *casting vote*, though it is usual for the mayor not to take part in council business, especially where there are strong political divisions on the council.

The following points should also be noted:

(a) His position is largely one of ceremony and prestige, and he is the first citizen of the borough and its chief representative.

(b) He has social and official precedence in the borough.

(c) The council may pay him such sum as they think fit, for when he acts as the personification of the authority considerable expenditure may arise. Salaries paid vary considerably, from approximately £200 to as high as £4,000 in the largest boroughs.

(d) He is an *ex officio* justice of the peace and acts as a link between local government and the administration of justice.

6. Comparative systems. The mayor in the English system is not an executive officer responsible for formulating policy or for leading the council. He is a social figurehead and by "gentlemen's agreement" is often appointed from each party in turn; while in office he will usually remain above politics.

In the *USA* the mayor is the chief executive in relation to the council, with independent powers and independent of the elected council. A similar position is occupied by the *Maire* in France and by the *Bürgermeister* in West Germany.

ALDERMEN

7. Nature of the office. The aldermanic system is a characteristic of English local government the value of which is much in doubt; it is confined to county councils, county boroughs and borough councils.

It was introduced by the *Municipal Corporations Act*, 1835, to form a long-serving nucleus on local authorities which would provide them with a degree of stability and continuity. Despite considerable and repeated opposition the system still prevails at the present day and forms a focal point of discontent.

8. Appointment. In counties and boroughs aldermen are elected by the councillors from among council members or from among persons qualified to serve on the council. They equal in number one-third of the council, with the exception of the Greater London Council and the London boroughs where the proportion is one-sixth. Their term of office is for six years and one-half retires every third year.

9. Role. They occupy no special role in local authority administration and their appointment stems from many motives, including personality, seniority, long service reward, political reward, and considerations of party politics.

10. Advantages of the system. Retention of the aldermanic system may be justified on the following grounds:

(a) *Stability.* It is claimed that the system contributes to local administration a measure of stability and accumulated experience which it would otherwise not have.

(b) *Ability.* Like co-option to committees, it can bring on to the council persons of experience and ability, who are unwilling to seek public election.

(c) *Status.* It gives local authorities an aura of status and antiquity. It appeals to the English passion for pageantry and ceremony.

11. Disadvantages of the system. In opposition to this rather ineffectual defence of the aldermanic system may be ranged the following persuasive arguments for its abolition, set out in **12** and **13** below.

12. Continuity already assured.

(a) *The prime motive.* The original motive for the creation of the system—to ensure stability and continuity of service— becomes rather irrelevant in the boroughs where only one-third of the members retire each year, thus preserving an experienced body in office after each election. The argument has more force in the counties where all retire every three years, but even here the probability is that a large proportion will be re-elected. (Besides, nobody urges the creation of a number of long-serving parliamentary politicians.)

(b) *The officers.* In any case the existence of professional and experienced officers of the council will produce continuity of programmes.

13. Other adverse features.

(a) *Undemocratic.* The system is undemocratic in that aldermen are not appointed by direct election and thus are not responsible to the electorate.

(b) *Motives.* The absence of firm criteria of selection leaves room for various motives for appointment and can lead to the bearing of grudges and discontent.

(c) *Used as a reward.* The suggested advantage of the system that it brings persons of ability into the council is not usually fulfilled in practice, and the office is generally regarded as a reward, rather than as a way of obtaining persons of ability.

(d) *Monopolies.* As appointments are based on seniority rather than ability there is a likelihood that aldermen will be re-elected until they retire of their own accord, and they may acquire dominance over the council, possibly through holding more committee chairmanships than is warranted by their real importance.

(e) *Possible abuse of system.* The system is open to abuse by irresponsible authorities, especially where dominated by party divisions, and may be used to defeat the true will of the electorate. This may occur through the bringing back of defeated councillors "through the back door" and the consolidation of party advantage by the appointment of aldermen.

NOTE: In Lewisham in 1959 the Labour Party had a minority of elected councillors, but this was turned into a majority by the number of Labour aldermen. By the use of the aldermanic votes and the casting vote of the mayor, a further increase of Labour members was achieved, directly against the expressed will of the electorate.

COUNCILLORS

14. Nature of the office. One of the main distinguishing features of English local government is the absence of full-time elected members, even in the largest authorities. The cult of the "amateur" which runs through a large part of English judicial and local government life stems from the nineteenth century. Desirable as unpaid service might have been under earlier conditions, its effectiveness in producing efficient membership of local authorities is seriously questioned today.

There exist in England and Wales over 40,000 unpaid local councillors directing the activities of over 2 million employees and controlling a budget of approaching £300 million per annum. It is therefore necessary to consider the type of person who becomes a local councillor, and possible reforms to improve the system.

15. Constitution.

(a) *County councils.* Councillors serve for three years and retire *en bloc.*

(b) *Boroughs and urban districts.* Three councillors represent each ward and are elected for a period of three years, with one-third retiring every year.

(c) *Rural districts.* The number of councillors for each electoral area is fixed by the county council, and elections are usually held every year with a fixed proportion of councillors retiring annually.

NOTE: A county council may, at the request of a district council, direct that the elections be held triennially.

(d) *Parishes* (and rural boroughs). Councillors are elected for a three-year period and retire *en bloc*.

(e) *London*. In both the Greater London Council and the London boroughs, councillors are elected for three years and retire *en bloc*.

RIGHTS AND DUTIES OF COUNCILLORS

16. Principal legal rights. There is a general absence of statutory or common law on the subject, and therefore to a large extent the rights and duties of councillors rest upon the conventions and practice of the individual local authority as regularised by its standing orders.

(a) *Executive power*. Local councillors have no executive power or lawful authority in their individual capacity, but only through the corporate entity of the council itself.

(b) *Allowances*. Local authorities are empowered to pay allowances to members in respect of financial loss, and for travelling and subsistence expenses. A rather low financial limit is laid down for the payment of allowances, which may only be paid where the member incurs expenses on *"approved duty."*

(c) *Inspection of documents*. A member has the right of access to such official documents, etc. as are necessary to enable him to carry out his duty, and the order of *mandamus* will lie to enforce the production of such documents. He does not, however, have the right to examine such documents out of mere curiosity.

17. Principal legal duties.

(a) *Attendance at council meetings*. A councillor who does not attend council meetings for six months, and is unable to offer a reasonable excuse for such absence is disqualified from serving on the council.

(b) *Disclosure of interest*. Where a member has a direct or indirect pecuniary interest in any matter before the council and is present at a meeting where such matter is discussed, he must disclose that interest and refrain from discussion and voting.

An *indirect* interest exists where the member is a member of a company, or any nominee of his is such a member, with which the contract under discussion is made or proposed to to be made, or if he is a partner or is in the employment of a person with whom the contract is made or to be made, or who has a direct pecuniary interest in the matter (*Local Government Act*, 1933, *s.* 76).

NOTE: If his beneficial interest in the company is through shares with a nominal value of £500, he must declare his interest but will not be precluded from speaking and voting.

PARTICULAR ISSUES

18. General. Even an utopian structure of local government with a scientific functional allocation would depend in the long run for its success on the quality of the persons running it. There has in recent years been a growing tendency to criticise councillors and to disparage their efforts, and the following points arising from the survey carried out by the Maud Committee throw light on the justification or otherwise of such criticism.

19. Maud Committee on the management of local government. The survey of the role of local councillors carried out by the committee revealed the following points:

(*a*) *Age structure.*

(i) 54 per cent of councillors were over 55, even though this age group made up only 33 per cent of the adult population.

(ii) 41 per cent were in the 35–54 age group, a figure corresponding to the proportion of that age group in the general population.

(*iii*) Only 5 per cent of male councillors were under the age of 35, compared with the proportion of this group in the general population of 27 per cent.

(*iv*) There was a particularly great preponderance of older councillors in rural districts (60 per cent over 55) and on county councils (nearly 70 per cent over 55).

NOTE: Although age of itself is not a defect in councillors, it is not unreasonable to assume that the older ones are more likely to be out of touch with the social climate of the era; unlikely to be "consumers" of local services; and will tend to be more conservative about welfare services, particularly education. This will result in maintenance of the *status quo* and reluctance to experiment.

(*b*) *Occupational representation.* The survey revealed an over-representation of certain occupational groupings, and in other cases severe under-representation, or even non-representation, in particular the following points emerged:

(*i*) Managers of small businesses (*i.e.* employing less than 25), comprised 25 per cent of all councillors, though only 7 per cent of the general population.

(*ii*) Farmer-employers and managers made up 16 per cent, while being 2 per cent of the population.

(*iii*) Skilled manual workers comprised 11 per cent, but made up 28 per cent of the general population.

(*iv*) Semi- and unskilled workers comprised 6 per cent of councillors, but 23 per cent of the general population. If further divided, unskilled workers and agricultural labourers made up 10 per cent of the population, but 1 per cent of councillors.

(*c*) *Social class.* Despite the difficulty of a satisfactory definition, it was clear that the working- and lower-middle class were severely under-represented.

(*d*) *Education.* Only 23 per cent of councillors have had further education (compared with 53 per cent of M.P.s). In future however it is likely that the proportion will rise, *e.g.* 21 per cent of present councillors under 35 have had university education.

20. Recommendations of the Maud Committee.

(*a*) *Retirement.* An age limit should be fixed for council service, and the matter should not be left to the discretion of the individual council.

(*b*) *Training.* The Local Authority Associations should seek to establish training courses for council members at universities or colleges.

(*c*) *Employers.* These should accept the fact that the release of their staff for work as members of local authorities is in the public interest.

(*d*) *Release.* Employers who do grant release should do so for at least 18 days a year.

(*e*) *Period of release.* This should not be deductible from holidays.

21. Why are better members not attracted?

It is pertinent to ask in a criticism of the membership of local authorities why in fact better quality members are not attracted into service, and it is suggested that the following points, or a combination of them, may be contributory factors:

(*a*) The need for *party allegiance.*

(*b*) The *time-consuming* nature of local administration.

(*c*) *Inconvenience.*

    (*d*) Lack of *discretionary freedom* of local authorities.

    (*e*) *Financial loss.*

    (*f*) *Unwillingness of employers* to release employees for council service.

In consequence a lack of balance has resulted in the structure of local councils both in age and in occupations.

PAYMENT OF COUNCILLORS

22. General. Possibly one of the most discussed problems about council membership is that of the advantages and the disadvantages of paying council members a salary, fees, etc. Any debate on such a matter is generally, however, emotionally clouded by fears of the loss of dignity resulting from professionalism, and the continuing belief in the nineteenth century concept of the local *"gentleman"* (albeit one with adequate time and money to devote himself to local administration). The following arguments may be advanced from both sides:

    (*a*) Arguments against payments.

      (*i*) Payment will result in the growth of a class of "local professional politicians" and the possibility of corruption. This argument however does not seem to be based on any factual evidence.

      (*ii*) Full-time paid members will become slaves of their party and dependent on supporting the party in order to remain in office.

      (*iii*) It will result in a loss of prestige and dignity (possibly a small price to pay for efficiency).

    (*b*) Arguments in favour of payments.

      (*i*) By creating a different type of local councillor it will restore public interest in local politics.

      (*ii*) Professionalism is needed in the twentieth century, and the concept of the "amateur" is now outdated.

      (*iii*) It will result in the growth of a skilled class of local administrators who would be able to counter-balance the growing power and domination of the central government officials.

      (*iv*) It will attract a better balanced representation of local councillors.

23. How much payment? Consideration must be given to the dangers of too high a rate of payment, which may result in the attraction of the wrong type of individual, and the danger of too low a rate of payment, which will do nothing to remedy the existing defects.

In France and the USA a living salary is not paid, and in Holland a system of payment is devised whereby a salary is paid to certain members in consideration of their giving personal oversight to services in their areas; similar in fact to the role of committee chairmen (*see* VI, **12, 13**).

It is felt that a balance could be obtained by the payment of reasonable expense allowances, plus an attendance allowance (as in the House of Lords) and the payment of special fees to committee chairmen.

24. Conclusion. The success of local administration depends therefore on the quality of its membership. Yet without adequate resources and without capable administrative leaders local representative government will not be successful. The cults of amateurism and parochialism are out of place in the twentieth century, and the role of local administration must eventually be viewed as a combination of wider powers given to elected authorities, but administered through trained, paid and effective local officials.

LOCAL GOVERNMENT OFFICERS

25. Introduction. *Laski* commented that "the whole difference between efficient and inefficient administration lies in the creative use of officials by elected persons." *Stamp* commented that "only skilled and trained officials can be relied upon to keep continuity, systems, impartial interpretation, and tradition and disinterested impetus."

Therefore in considering local government officials it is important not only to view them from constitutional and functional aspects, but also from the standpoint of their effective role in local administration.

26. General. The work of a local authority is based on the inter-relationship of paid, trained officials and the elected representatives working together through the committee system (*see* VI, **10–13**). In the context of modern administration it is vital that the work of local authorities be executed by paid and trained officers who have accumulated the necessary experience.

c

27. Appointment of officers. In general councils are responsible for their internal administrative structure and may appoint "such officers as they think fit for the efficient discharge of the functions of the council." In addition certain statutory appointments are mandatory, and the central government possesses the power and the duty to approve of certain appointments and a degree of interference over such matters as the dismissal of certain officers.

28. Statutory appointments. Counties, county boroughs and district councils must appoint a clerk, a treasurer, a medical officer of health, and a surveyor. (This does not apply to rural districts.) All authorities except counties must appoint at least one public health inspector.

In addition counties and county boroughs must appoint a chief education officer and a children's officer.

Coroners, public analysts, shops inspectors, weights and measures inspectors, registration and returning officers for local elections must be appointed by all local authorities responsible for the performance of such duties.

Parish councils must appoint a clerk and a treasurer, but only the former may be paid.

NOTE: Even though an authority is only required to make certain appointments it will in practice make considerably more: *e.g.* in addition to the town clerk an authority will usually appoint in his department a deputy town clerk, assistant solicitors, legal and conveyancing clerks, committee clerks and various clerical personnel.

29. Qualifications. No qualifications are prescribed for officers except in the case of medical officers of health, and public health inspectors. The clerks, treasurers and surveyors are merely required to be " fit" persons.

30. Statutory interference.

(*a*) *Choice of officers.* As a general rule an authority has a discretion as to the officers it will appoint, subject to certain exceptions:

(*i*) A *local education authority* must consult the Secretary of State before appointing a chief education officer, and from the submitted list of candidates the Secretary may remove any he does not consider suitable.

(*ii*) The same applies with *children's officers*.

(b) *Dismissal.* Generally officers hold their appointments at the pleasure of the council, though matters concerning notice, etc. will be regulated by the conditions of service of officers laid down by the council. However, the clerk and medical officer of health of a county council, public analysts, and medical officers of health and public health inspectors of boroughs, urban and rural districts cannot be dismissed without the *consent of the Minister.*

31. Departmental structure. Local authorities are generally organised on a departmental basis, with each department administering a service or groups of interrelated services. Each department will be headed by a chief officer and will be responsible to a committee.

Organisation may be on a vertical basis with a department responsible for the related aspects of a particular service, *e.g.* health, whereas other departments will be horizontal in that they will be responsible for aspects which cut across all services. The principal horizontal departments will be the town clerk's and the treasurer's departments, both of which deal with subjects concerning all other departments, *e.g.* the giving of legal advice and the internal auditing of accounts.

32. Principal horizontal departments.

(a) *The clerk's department.* This is probably the senior department on any local authority and is the repository of legal and administrative functions. It deals mainly with such matters as the giving of legal advice; the servicing of committees through its committee clerks; legal transactions such as the sale of property; public relations; and the keeping of council records. (It will usually also house the establishment section.)

(b) *The treasurer's department.* This deals with council finance and accounts; costing; internal audit; budget preparation; wages; and the legality of payments.

33. Principal other departments.

(a) *Engineer and surveyor's department.* This deals with such matters as construction and maintenance of buildings, highways, sewage works, etc. (A county council will usually have a separate highways department because of its greater responsibilities.)

(b) *Chief education officer's department.* Responsibility for schools and further education establishments; appointment of

teachers; examinations; school development and related education matters.

(c) *Medical officer of health*. His office has general powers of
oversight over the public and personal health services.

(d) *Housing*. Responsibility for the provision of council
housing and its maintenance and the dealing with unfit premises.

(e) *Public health*. Environmental health conditions, sanitation, sewers, statutory nuisances, etc., in many cases working
through the agency of public health inspectors.

(f) *Planning department*. This is responsible for formulation
and operation of the development plan, and through the plan
for the control of development.

34. Role of the clerk. The clerk is the principal officer of the
council, and acts as its chief executive and administrative
officer. He is responsible as a result of this to the council for
the overall working of the local authority. He fulfils the role of
co-ordinator of departments as well as acting as legal adviser,
secretary and spokesman for the council. His importance is
emphasised by the need for a single overall authority responsible for co-ordinating the work of the various departments in
order to achieve maximum efficiency.

The tendency to regard legal qualifications as a prerequisite
to the appointment has been continuously questioned, and a
tendency has developed to place more emphasis on administrative ability (*Onslow Committee*, 1934). To insist upon legal
qualifications, it is argued, would exclude "persons of high
administrative ability whose experience has been gained in
other work." For example in 1965 Newcastle upon Tyne
appointed a high executive of the Ford Motor Company to act
as the "Principal City Officer." In other authorities, too, an
increase in non-legal appointments is noted.

35. Role of the officers. The administrative context of local
government results in the development of a relationship between the officers and the council which resembles that in
other administrative spheres: *i.e.* the paid official carries out
the work, while the council decides and controls policy and
holds the purse strings.

However, the local government relationship is clouded by
the outdated attitude that it is the responsibility of the elected
representative to be responsible for detailed control of administration. The officer being a trained and experienced individual

should be given the right to advise on policy, as he is in the best position to measure the impact of existing policy; he has knowledge as to the adequacy of resources; and he has the experience and the foresight to enable him to estimate the future effects of policy decisions. But it is the duty of the council to keep the balance and to prevent over-ambition on the part of the officers.

36. Relations between officers and committees. The officer is responsible for presenting his report to the appropriate committee on work executed and matters requiring attention, and his suggestions and recommendations. The committee should establish the dividing line between matters of principle which is its responsibility, and matters of management and execution which it should entrust to the discretion of the officer. It is only by the correct drawing of this dividing line that officers can be used to the best purpose and will achieve greater satisfaction from local government service. (*See also* role of committee chairmen, VI, **12, 13.**)

37. The officers and the public. Local government officers owe both a duty to the local authority and to the public: *e.g.* it was held in the case of *A. G.* v. *De Winton* (1906) that the treasurer is under a duty to disobey orders of the council which are illegal. The decision also emphasises that the treasurer is a trustee of public funds and therefore has a responsibility for public welfare. Similar views have been expressed regarding the duties of the clerk.

In addition to this legal obligation the officer is the principal means through which the public have contact with the local authority, and, as he is a servant of the public through the agency of the local authority, his attitude and ability will have important effects on public confidence in local authorities.

THE CITY-MANAGER

38. Position in the USA. At present over 2,000 authorities in the USA have adopted the city-manager system of administration, and a large number more adopt some variation of the system. In addition to its rapid development in the USA the system is also used in West Germany and Ireland.

39. The system. A municipal council, which is generally much smaller than its UK counterpart, is elected to perform the legislative responsibilities of local administration. The council when elected appoints a professional city-manager, who acts as chief administrative officer under the theoretical direction of the council. However, such direction is comparatively limited, and the manager assumes responsibility for the functions of city management and is generally independent of the council as regards day-to-day administration. He is the chief executive and is responsible for executing the council's policy, for financial aspects of the administration, the supervision of budgetary preparation, and for the scrutinising of supplementary estimates.

40. Advantages of the office. The advantages must be seen in the context of a differing structure of administration, involving an absence of committees and a smaller council. The system was deliberately designed as an experiment in the application of business management techniques to local government, with the council representing the board of directors, and the city-manager the managing director. The system has proved very successful in medium-sized American cities and the following advantages have been claimed:

(a) *Flexibility.* By giving the city-manager the power of re-arrangement, creation and abolition of departments, and the appointment and dismissal of officers, changes in the administrative structure of local government are easily made.

(b) *Professionalised management.* This is also achieved.

(c) *Effective co-ordination.* This is rendered easier by the concentration of executive power in a single person.

(d) *Simplicity.* The system is simple, and also provides speedy decision-taking.

(e) *Responsibility.* This is ensured by making the manager strictly accountable to the council, which has the power of dismissal.

NOTE: There has, however, been a rapid turnover in city-managers in the USA. This probably points to a rigidity of attitude on both sides which must reduce efficiency.

41. Is it desirable in England? The system is generally opposed in England and Wales on the following grounds:

(a) It would require an administrative upheaval to put into

practice, involving the abolition of committees and a reduction in the size of councils.

(b) There would be a diminution of democratic control.

(c) It would lead to the subordination of chief officers.

REFORM PROPOSALS

42. Mallaby Committee. The Committee, in its Report on the *Staffing of Local Government* published in 1967, made the following recommendations regarding "the existing methods of recruiting local government officers; of using them; and what changes might help local authorities get the best services from their officers and help the officers to give it."

(a) *Recruitment.* The need to recruit more graduates was emphasised, and greater liaison with universities and colleges to do this. Good training schemes must be introduced to attract school leavers.

(b) *Career prospects.* There is a need for equalising the opportunities of the school leaver and the graduate, and for establishing the proper place of the technician alongside professional officers. There should also be greater opportunities for lay administrative officers.

(c) *Selection procedure.* The use is urged of small panels for the selection of chief officers coupled with the use of outside assessors. Principal officers should be responsible for the appointment of their own staffs.

(d) *Training.* Training facilities should be provided and officers encouraged to use them. These should be the responsibility of the clerk. Full-time courses should be established, induction training encouraged, and allowance made for trainees in fixing establishments.

(e) *Use of staff.* The need to use professional resources, the giving of discretion, and where suitable the use of private resources was stressed. Recommendations were also made on internal organisation and favouring the encouragement of *staff nobility*.

43. The Maud Committee. In considering how "in the light of modern conditions local government might best continue to attract and retain people of the calibre necessary to ensure its maximum effectiveness" the committee made the following observation on the role of the officer:

(a) *Ultimate control.* This must rest with the elected officers.

(b) *Key decisions.* These are to be taken by the members.

(c) *Review.* Members *periodically to review* the progress and performance of the services.

(d) *Staff work.* The officers are to provide the necessary staff work and advice, so that members may set objectives and take decisions about achieving them.

(e) *Day-to-day work.* Officers are to be responsible for *day-to-day administration* case-work decisions and routine inspection and control.

(f) *Special problems.* Officers are to be responsible for identifying and isolating particular problems which in their opinion have such implications that the members must consider and decide upon them.

44. Evidence to Royal Commission on Local Government.
The following evidence on the role of officers was given to the commission:

(a) *The Royal Institute of Chartered Surveyors.* The Institute emphasised the need to create authorities capable of employing staff of a higher quality. The creation of larger authorities would provide the opportunity of employing high calibre staff, and the provision of proper training facilities. It also urged a proper recognition of the status of professional staff. Also recommended was the appointment of a general manager who should be the unchallenged head of administration, with principal officers having wide discretionary powers.

(b) *The Institute of Municipal Treasurers and Accountants.* The Institute felt that the multiplicity of authorities and the division of functions resulted in inefficiency in the use of staff resources. It felt that regional posts would offer a greater challenge, status and influence. It would prevent the wastage of top-level staff and introduce a greater element of dynamism into the role of the officer.

PROGRESS TEST 5

1. What are the qualifications and disqualifications for membership of local authorities? **(1, 2)**
2. What are the roles of mayor and chairman? **(3–5)**
3. How does the mayor operate in foreign systems? **(6)**
4. What are aldermen and how are they appointed? **(7–9)**
5. What justification is there for retaining the aldermanic system? **(10)**
6. What are the disadvantages of the aldermanic system? **(12–13)**
7. What is the nature of the office of councillor? **(14)**
8. How are local authorities constituted? **(3, 7, 15)**

9. What are the principal legal rights and duties of councillors? (**16, 17**)

10. What did the Maud Committee Report reveal about the age and occupational structure of councillors? (**18, 19**)

11. What recommendations did the Maud Committee make on council membership? (**20**)

12. What factors operate to reduce willingness to serve on councils? (**21**)

13. What are the arguments for and against the payment of councillors? (**22–24**)

14. To what extent does the central government interfere with the appointment of officers? (**30**)

15. Outline the departmental structure of a local authority. (**31–33**)

16. What is the role of the clerk? (**34**)

17. What is the role of the local government officer? (**26, 27, 36, 37**)

18. What do you understand by the office of city-manager in the USA, and what are its advantages? (**38–40**)

19. Is it desirable in England? (**41**)

20. What were the principal recommendations of the Mallaby Committee? (**42**)

21. What were the principal recommendations of the Maud Committee on the personnel of local authorities? (**43**)

CHAPTER VI

THE DISPOSAL OF LOCAL AUTHORITY BUSINESS

GENERAL FEATURES

1. General aspects. The effective disposal of the business of a local authority cannot be regarded as the single duty of any individual or group of individuals, but will only be achieved through effective and efficient co-ordination and co-operation between the council itself, its committees and its full-time officers.

The large amount of business dealt with at the present day has produced a system where each has his own particular role to fulfil, and has called for the development of a method for unifying the individual roles. Before dealing with the details of each of the constituent parts, the following general picture may be presented.

2. Role of the council. The council, as the principal body of the local authority, is primarily responsible for policy decisions, holding the balance between individual departments and committees, and for discussion of matters of general importance.

3. Role of the committees. The role of the committees is the detailed consideration of the various aspects of local authority work, and the formulation of proposals to be submitted to the council, which, if adopted, will form part of the council's overall policy.

In addition the committees form the basic and vital link between the elected representatives and the officers of the council concerned with the actual administration of a particular service. The committees are also responsible for control and supervision over the departments of the council. Also in certain cases the committees are empowered to exercise certain functions of the council itself (*see* **11**(*b*) below).

4. Role of the officers. Although basically concerned with the administration of the council's policy decisions, the officers are in the best position to determine the actual effects of them. Their role of necessity thus ceases to be merely executive, and involves liaison with the committees and the giving of advice on questions of policy and practice.

5. Standing orders. As mentioned above, the relations between the council, its committees, its departments and its officers all require the closest co-ordination, control and stimulus to co-operation in order to achieve efficient administration. For this reason the practice of a local authority, as evolved from experience, is usually embodied in standing orders, which may be regarded as the rules of the council for the efficient running of its administrative system. Such a system may be periodically reviewed in the light of changing circumstances and requirements.

THE COUNCIL

6. General. Most of the business of the council consists in formulating policy. This is largely dealt with by examining the reports of the committees and their recommendations. The great volume of work facing the council requires the development of an expeditious procedure, and although this must be more formal than that of the committees (due to its larger size) effective rules are generally formulated.

However, the council is the outward and public embodiment of the local authority, and as a result certain rules are in force to ensure that its work is open to the public.

7. Working rules.

(a) *Meetings.* County, borough, district and parish councils must meet once a year, or if there is no parish council, twice a year. However, in practice meetings will be held more often, and weekly meetings in larger authorities are not uncommon. In any case a minimum number of members may require a meeting to be held if the chairman at their request fails to call one.

(b) *Prior public notice.* This must be given specifying the business to be transacted.

(c) *Minutes.* These must be kept, and they are open to inspection by the electors on payment of a fee (with the right also to take extracts).

(d) *Attendance.* There must be a *quorum* (usually one-third or one-quarter of the members) before a meeting can take place.

(e) *Accounts.* These must be open to inspection free of charge.

(f) *Voting.* Records of voting and how individuals cast their votes must be kept.

(g) *Standing orders.* These must be complied with.

8. Rights of the public and press. Under the *Public Bodies (Admission to Meetings) Act*, 1960, the meetings of local authorities are required to be open to the public. However, power is given to exclude the press and public from meetings, whenever publicity would be prejudicial to the public interest because of the confidential nature of the business to be discussed, or for other special reasons stated in the resolution excluding the public and arising from the nature of the business. For example where the council is to consider information from persons or bodies other than the council, committees, officers, etc., or where allegations against an individual member or officer are made.

9. Maud Committee survey. A survey conducted on behalf of the Maud Committee revealed that two out of three citizens find out about local authority work through the local press. The practice of excluding the press appears to be infrequent, and in fact there is a growing practice, despite the absence of legal obligation, to admit journalists to committee meetings— a practice supported by successive Ministers and by the national political parties.

One-half of all authorities do not admit the press to any committee meetings; 40 per cent to some; and 10 per cent to all. Bristol even allows the press to attend the meetings of subcommittees. For the release of information to the press, 33 per cent of all councils place an embargo on council papers until after the meeting (probably because few authorities outside London employ public relations officers).

THE COMMITTEE SYSTEM

10. Disposal of business through committees. The limitations imposed by time, by complexity, and by the unwieldiness of the council mean that the main burden of the council's duties are delegated in some form or other to smaller committees.

Apart from statutory committees, which an authority is bound to appoint, local authorities may appoint committees for general or specific purposes as they think fit. Membership of a committee is fixed by the council, except in limited cases such as the finance and education committees; and the general structure of the committees, their duties, their relationships, their powers and their co-ordination is the responsibility of the individual council concerned.

11. General principles. It is correct to say that, despite its disadvantages and limitations, the committee system is at the heart of English local government, and that proposals for reforming the internal workings of local government must centre on the committee structure.

There are three general principles under which the business of a committee may be allocated:

(a) *Advisory.* The council may refer specific matters to committees, and in such cases the decisions of the committee are not effective until confirmed by the council. They then become decisions of the council, and not of the individual committee which is acting in an advisory capacity.

(b) *Executive.* The council may delegate specific matters, and in such a case the decision of the committee is effective forthwith and without the necessity of endorsement by the council. Under the *Local Government Act*, 1933 (*s.* 85), an authority is empowered to delegate any of its functions to a committee with or without restriction or conditions, *except* the power to levy a rate, issue a precept, or raise a loan.

NOTE: Excessive delegation would result in a weakening of the work of the council and a loss of its true role of democratic representation. Accordingly close control of such power is vital to the continuance of local democracy.

(c) *Mandatory.* In certain cases the authority may not act until a report of a committee is made.

12. Main role of committee chairman. The chairman of a committee must explain more fully its proposals, resolutions and recommendations to the council, and will be the spokesman of the committee in debates on its work and reports. His opening speeches to the council will be the means by which the public is kept informed.

13. Committee chairman's other duties. He is in a unique position in that his powers go far beyond controlling his committee's debates. There is a need to increase the contact between officers and the committee, quite apart from committee meetings. This is provided by the close relations of officers with the chairman of committees. Urgent matters may arise in cases where it is impractical to call a committee meeting, and then the officer involved will usually consult the committee chairman and act upon his advice and direction. The chairman is thus responsible for *feeling* the committee's mood, and being able to rely upon subsequent confirmation by the committee and if necessary by the council.

The chairman is thus the "eyes and ears" of his committee and knows more than does the ordinary member, as he will be kept acquainted with the work of the department by its chief officer. His position has no legal authority and depends on personality, though this may have the danger of creating "dictatorship."

Finally, it may be said that his position is somewhat analagous to that of a minister of the Crown, and that he is responsible for his committee and department.

THE COMMITTEE STRUCTURE

14. Statutory committees. A large number of statutes require a local authority to set up committees for specific purposes, to make provision for the membership of such committees, and to provide that all matters relating to a certain service be referred to the appropriate committee.

Important examples of such statutory committees are:

(*a*) *County councils.* Every county council must have a finance committee; an education committee; and a children's committee.

(*b*) *County borough.* Every county borough (and county) must appoint a welfare committee and a health committee.

(*c*) Every *borough* must have a watch committee.

NOTE: To these and other statutory committees must be referred all business relating to a particular function or service, and as a general rule the council may not act until receiving a report from the committee concerned.

15. Membership of statutory committees. The local authority may be given statutory direction as to the membership of such committees: *e.g.* the provisions establishing education, maternity, child welfare, and housing committees require that co-option be made of persons representing particular interest involved, or persons with special knowledge and experience, or for the inclusion of a minimum number of women. In the case of the finance committee co-option is statutorily prohibited.

16. Other committees. Apart from statutory committees, local authorities have a general discretion as to the structure of their committee system. Generally such committees as they appoint may be divided into:

(*a*) *Standing committees.* These are permanent committees dealing with a branch of the local authority's business. They may be further subdivided into:

(*i*) Horizontal committees which deal with aspects of a local authority's business, cutting across all or most of the services. The principal horizontal committee is the finance committee which must determine the actual amount to be spent by any particular service, and thus obtains a position of *de facto* dominance over all other committees. Other horizontal committees will include supply and establishment committees.

(*ii*) Vertical committees which deal with the remaining general aspects of a service: *e.g.* health, housing, highways and education committees.

NOTE: The vertical committees may recommend the allocation of resources, establishment, etc. in their own favour, but ultimate decisions must be made through the horizontal committees.

(*b*) *Ad hoc committees.* These are set up to deal with some specific terminable aspect of local authority business.

17. Sub-committees. From time to time a standing committee may wish to appoint a sub-committee on either a standing or special basis. Care must be taken not only in defining the terms of reference of the sub-committee, especially where *delegation* is involved, but also in avoiding a proliferation of such committees. A balance must be struck between creating a sub-committee at random to meet every difficulty which may crop up in the course of the business of the main committee, and the tendency to be reluctant to appoint such committees, so that the main committee is overburdened with trivialities and time-consuming details.

18. The role of the finance committee. The finance committee, as the most important horizontal committee, deals with the control of finance and thus directs the work of the committees. Although it is not universally mandatory, it is the general practice for all authorities to appoint a finance committee. The committee will be involved in watching over all other departments, and in prior consultation over such matters as supplementary estimates. The committee may itself be composed of committee chairmen, but this may be undesirable as it may lead to domination by one party, and to inter-departmental bickering.

NOTE: Of less importance, but still of considerable effect, in balancing inter-departmental claims are the supply and establishment committees.

CO-OPTION

19. General. The fear that democratically constituted local authorities might not be adequate to run the specialised services involved in local government administration may be met by the following considerations:

(a) *The officers* who run the services are experts.

(b) *Committee members* are likely to specialise in a particular service or group of services, and thus obtain a general knowledge of a service to which they may contribute the application of common-sense.

(c) There is *a power to co-opt* outside persons to serve on the committees and to use the specialised knowledge of such persons in this way.

With the exception of the finance committee a local authority may add to any of its committees persons who are not members of the council, up to a limit of one-third of the elected members.

20. Disadvantages of co-option. Co-option appears generally out of favour with local authorities, and insufficient use is made of the power for the following reasons:

(*a*) It is considered undemocratic.

(*b*) It is open to abuse by the appointment of persons on political grounds.

(*c*) It may result in the introduction of fractious elements who have no direct responsibility to the electorate.

21. Advantages of co-option. It is felt that there is a need to encourage the use of co-option, but at the same time it is felt that apart from organised pressure groups it is doubtful whether there are any genuine "non-party" people who are prepared to devote time to the job.

(*a*) There are developing local groups for education, planning, preservation of amenities, and some minority services such as mental health, whose energy could well be used for local purposes.

(*b*) Co-option would help to bridge the gap which exists between the council and the public.

(*c*) It provides a valuable addition in expertise, in technical knowledge, and in bringing out the consumer and user aspects of a service. Provided that the elected members are in control of all committees, which in fact they are bound to be, it is hard to see any force in the claim that co-option is undemocratic.

(*d*) Non-party members would be able to view issues with greater detachment.

CO-ORDINATION BETWEEN COMMITTEES

22. Nature of the problem. A basic task of a local authority using committees is the control and co-ordination of their work. The dividing of functions and the consequent development of functional specialisation tends to give rise to "departmentalism." This may mean that members of one committee may lose sight of its true role in the administrative context of the local authority, and thus may adapt an isolationist view of its powers and responsibilities.

23. General control by the council. A major task of the council in achieving efficient co-ordination and control is that of *clearly defining* the functions and the powers of each committee and sub-committee. The local authority exercises control in that it *chooses the members* of committees and:

(*a*) It lays down the rules governing the relationship of the various committees.

(*b*) It controls their spending.

(*c*) It sets limits upon their freedom of action.

24. Other methods of control. The council may also exercise control through:

(*a*) *A general purposes committee.* This may be appointed to deal with matters affecting the general policy of the council's services as a whole. To this committee may be referred matters affecting more than one committee, so that the general purposes committee is enabled to become a co-ordinating agency, and to obtain and to reconcile the views of the individual committees concerned. It is a usual practice to appoint committee chairmen to sit upon such a committee.

(*b*) *Periodical reports.* The council may require and receive periodical reports from the committees, reserve to itself the more important points and limit the committees to the giving of advice.

(*c*) *Reserving finance.* By reserving control of finance the council may keep to itself the power to review all the functions and work of committees, and to co-ordinate their functions from a general point of view.

(*d*) *Formal approval.* In cases where formal council approval is required for a committee decision the power of the council is confirmed, and the relationship between committees is made clear.

25. Control through chairmen and officials. Methods of control also include the following:

(*a*) *Control through committee chairmen.* The unique position of these individuals enables them by prior consultation to establish mutually acceptable lines of conduct for their respective committees.

(*b*) *Co-ordination by officials.* By keeping committees informed in cases where his duties are affected by more than one committee, an official can estimate the practical effect of committee decisions and the interrelated problem of such committees can be co-ordinated.

(*c*) *The committee clerks.* The secretarial role of the clerk of the council and of the committee clerks leads to a standardisation of procedure, which is considered at regular meetings of chief officers.

APPRAISAL OF THE COMMITTEE SYSTEM

26. Main advantages. The following are the main advantages of the committee system:

(a) *Full coverage.* It makes for a fuller coverage of the work of the council than would be possible if all matters were left to the council itself. It thus permits a division of functions into the making of policy by the council and the administration of it by the individual committees.

(b) *Specialisation.* Division of work among the members leads them to attain a degree of specialisation in a narrow range of subjects. This adds to the personal satisfaction of members and increases their contribution to the work of the council. It thus reduces the *amateur* aspect of local authority administration by assisting the development of a reasonably skilled and informed elected body.

(c) *Control by elected representatives.* Specialisation, in addition to increasing efficiency, enables elected members to achieve a greater degree of *constructive* control over officers than would otherwise be possible.

(d) *Contact with officials.* The system brings into contact the chief officers and the members of the authority, and unifies their specialised knowledge and common sense, thus resulting in more efficient administration coupled with public responsibility.

27. Other advantages. Other advantages include the following:

(a) *Participation by members.* It increases the reality of democratic participation by enabling the individual member to make a greater contribution. Such members will get more chance of speaking in committee, and will be concerned with the more practical aspects of local administration, rather than with feats of oratory.

(b) *Co-option: see* **19** above.

(c) *Opinions heard.* It increases the chances of a cross-section of opinion being heard.

(d) *Relaxed atmosphere.* The absence of the press, the smaller numbers, and the more informal nature of committee meetings encourage a more relaxed discussion of business than is possible in council meetings.

28. Disadvantages of the system. While it is generally accepted that some form of committee organisation is vital, various criticisms of it are made. These are given in **29** and **30** below.

29. Decreased efficiency.

(a) *Delays.* The chain of delegation and the long delays occasioned by the infrequency of committee meetings makes the committee system an unsuitable vehicle for day-to-day administration. Of course this can be alleviated by close co-operation between committee chairmen and officers.

(b) *Proliferation.* The demands of council work may lead to a proliferation of committees and sub-committees, and the advantages of specialisation will be lost by the overspreading of duties. It will lead to greater calls upon the time of members and increased reluctance to serve. Over-division will make efficient decisions difficult, as the need for co-ordination will increase; it will also reduce the time a member has to spend in maintaining personal relations with the electorate.

(c) *Paper work.* As the number of committees and sub-committees grows, the burden of assimilating the output of "paper" increases. This takes a disproportionately large part of the time of council members, officers and committee clerks.

(d) *Administration.* The use of committees and sub-committees to increase efficiency is often rendered ineffective by the tendency to create them in order to give committee chairmanships, rather than to achieve efficient administration. The setting up of separate committees for each service will lead to departmentalism, pride of office, and consequent ill-feeling, when amalgamation or grouping of committees is necessary.

30. Other disadvantages.

(a) *Isolationist attitudes.* There is a danger that over-specialisation and the granting of too much delegated power to committees will result in an isolationist attitude and an intolerance of other services. This may lead to constant friction, deliberate lack of co-ordination and loss of efficiency.

(b) *Failure to co-opt.* (*See* **19** above.)

(c) *Monopoly of power.* There is a danger of monopolisation by the dominant party, especially in the case of committee chairmanships.

(d) *Nineteenth century attitudes.* The excessive use of committees for controlling administration in detail is undesirable at the present day. The nineteenth century attitude that democratic control involved detailed control by the elected members is not practicable in the light of the needs of modern administration.

(e) *Lack of publicity.* The general non-admission of public and press to meeting of committees and sub-committees tends to throw a cloak over their proceedings and consequently decreases the amount of interest felt by the public. This engenders a distrust and lack of interest in local affairs.

THE OUTLOOK FOR REFORM

31. The Maud Committee. The Maud Committee drew the following conclusions on the present internal organisation of local authorities:

(a) *The system of administration.* This has its roots in the nineteenth century preoccupation with the direct and detailed responsibility of local leaders for local affairs. Although this was justified where there was little government interference and a lack of professional officers, it is irrelevant at the present day.

(b) *A distinction* must be drawn between the advantages of *deliberation* in committee, and the disadvantages of *detailed administration* by committees.

32. Advantages of committees. The Maud Committee concluded that committees were of advantage in that:

(a) They led to a better chance of the right decision being taken.

(b) They led to wider participation in the work of the authority.

(c) They represented wider interests.

(d) They are a safeguard against bureaucracy and unresponsive administration.

(e) They keep officers in close touch with political and public opinion.

33. Disadvantages of committees. The Maud Committee concluded that they were disadvantageous, however, on the following grounds:

(a) The growth of the work of authorities and its increased technical complexity has resulted in committees being unable to supervise adequately.

(b) The system wastes time and causes delays and frustration.

(c) It does not encourage discrimination between major objectives and the means of attaining them.

(*d*) The increase in paper work wastes time, and tends to discourage certain individuals from serving.

(*e*) The system produces a loose confederation involving the spreading of responsibility for taking decisions. Leadership and responsibility are not easily identified, with consequent difficulties of co-ordination.

(*f*) It is not adaptable to changing circumstances.

34. Maud Committee reform principles. The basic principles of internal organisation should be:

(*a*) *Effective and efficient management* under the direction and control of the members.

(*b*) *Clear leadership* and responsibility to be defined between members and officers.

(*c*) *An organisation* which presents to the public an understandable form of government.

(*d*) *Responsiveness* to public needs.

35. Maud Committee reform proposals. The Committee recommended that the following reforms should be made in order to implement its guiding principles:

(*a*) *A clear division of labour.* This must be arranged between the members and the officers of a local authority, to allow the members to settle policy, whilst allowing the officers to take all but the most important decisions.

(*b*) *Committees.* These should be *deliberative* and not be concerned with the detailed day-to-day management of a service.

(*c*) *Reduction in numbers.* There should be as few committees as possible consistent with efficient management. *"Grouping"* of committees should be encouraged, *e.g.* the committees of a local authority dealing with health and welfare services should become a single committee. Also there should be a reduction of sub-committees.

(*d*) *Departments.* These should also be subject to *grouping* arrangements.

(*e*) *Management board.* There should be a salaried management board concerned with co-ordination of committees, scrutiny of committee work before submission to the council, etc. Such a board could also submit *"white papers"* to the council.

36. Reactions to the Maud Report. The Council of the London Borough of Bexley set up a six-man working party to study the Maud Report. The working party has resulted in a complete reorganisation of the council structure. The number

of committees has been reduced from 51 to 13, and a new *policy committee* has been established to make recommendations to other committees. Where, however, a similar proposal was made by the City Manager of Newcastle upon Tyne, it was rejected by the council.

37. Comparative view. The general position in foreign local government systems is the same as in the English system: the supremacy of the elected council is the main point. However, the main variation is that a large number of such systems use an *executive* with responsibility for carrying out the decisions of the council, preparation of council business, supervision of the departments, and acting as an intermediary through which all business passes between the council and the departments.

PROGRESS TEST 6

1. Outline the role of the council, the committees and the officers in the disposal of local authority business.   **(1–5)**

2. What are the importance of standing orders?   **(5)**

3. Consider the rights of the public and the press to attend council and committee meetings.   **(8, 9)**

4. What is the committee system?   **(10)**

5. What forms may the system take?   **(11, 14–16)**

6. When should sub-committees be appointed?   **(17)**

7. What is the special role of the finance committee?   **(18)**

8. What is meant by co-option?   **(19)** What are its advantages and disadvantages?   **(20, 21)**

9. How is co-ordination between committees achieved?   **(22–25)**

10. What is the special role of the committee chairmen?   **(12, 13)**

11. What are the advantages and disadvantages of the committee systems?   **(26–30)**

12. What conclusions did the Maud Committee draw on the present-day internal organisation of local authorities?   **(31–32)**

13. What were the principal recommendations of the Maud Committee on internal organisations?   **(34, 35)**

14. What general forms do foreign systems take?   **(37)**

CHAPTER VII

CENTRAL GOVERNMENT CONTROL

GENERAL CONSIDERATIONS

1. Definition. Central government control of local authorities is interpreted to mean the control of such authorities by the central administrative departments of the state.

2. Characteristics. The following are the general characteristics of the control exercised over local authorities in England and Wales:

(*a*) *Absence of sole control.* There is no Ministry of the Interior able to regulate local authorities to suit the will of the government of the day. Although, as will be seen, certain central departments are given what appear to be overall powers of control, it will be clear that in practice administrative control springs from certain well-defined sources of power.

(*b*) *No centrally controlled officials.* There are no local government officials directly under the control of the central government, as for example in France, where the *maire* acts as a member of the state administration and can be instructed to perform certain tasks by the *préfet*, who in turn is under the direct control of the Minister of the Interior.

(*c*) *Independent revenue.* Rates provide local authorities with an independent source of revenue, and as a result they have a slightly greater control over their own destinies, subject to their acting within the law. However, as will become apparent, the increasing reliance on the central government for financial assistance has substantially reduced the strength of this independence.

(*d*) *Formal control.* All formal central government control must stem from some statutory power, and the intervention of the central departments must be justified within the framework of the law.

(*e*) *Informal control.* Despite the need for legal authorisation of powers of control, attention must be paid to the vital field of informal control.

3. All-pervading influence. It is suggested that the conclusion which may be drawn from studying the subsequent detailed analysis of central government control is that local authorities are subjected to such a massive all-pervading influence from the central government that there is a tendency for local authorities to feel psychologically dependent upon it. Thus they are subservient even in fields in which they have received or maintain a degree of independence: *e.g.* when a problem confronts a local authority its almost automatic reaction is to seek ministerial guidance.

DEVELOPMENT OF CENTRAL CONTROL

4. Early development. The period after the *Reform Act*, 1832, saw Parliament assume a different character, and heralded a period of responsibility and innovating legislation. Parliament sought internal reform to avoid the legislative delays characteristic of the eighteenth century. It also realised its responsibility to the electorate for the conduct of all national and local affairs, and as a result sought means whereby ministerial responsibility could be adequately shown in local affairs. The basic features influencing the relations between central and local government during the middle of the nineteenth century were as follows:

(*a*) *Relief of destitution.* The new industrial areas highlighted this need during a period of *laissez-faire* when local control was difficult to achieve.

(*b*) *Health.* It was necessary to develop health safeguards in a period of little medical knowledge and apathy on the part of local authorities.

(*c*) *The search for responsible and competent government.*

(*d*) *Progressive authorities.* The activities of progressive authorities in the field of sanitation paved the way for Parliament to assume responsibility for acts of administration.

(*e*) *Control.* The realisation of the need to control the occurrences of daily life.

5. The Poor Law Commissioners. The policies adopted by the Poor Law Commissioners in the period 1834–1847 determined many of the techniques of central control which were adopted up to 1929. The principal features of the Poor Law system in relation to central control may be classified as follows:

(*a*) *Central regulation.* Regulations were laid down by the central authority and supported by a large volume of circulars and directions to the local boards. This had the tendency to reduce local discretion.

(b) *Control of local officials.*

(c) *Inspection and audit.* A complete system of inspection, audit and financial control was instituted.

6. Control of health. The General Board of Health established in 1848, and that established in 1854, suffered from defects basically attributable to the weakening of their proposed powers of control during the passage of their constituting Acts, *e.g.* local boards were allowed to appoint their own auditors; they had control over their officials; and no satisfactory system of financial aid existed. The Board also suffered from the absence of trained officials.

7. The Local Government Board, 1871. The Royal Sanitary Commission (1868) recommended the establishment of a single central authority responsible for the associated matters of destitution and public health. The basic view was that such a board could reshape local administration from the chaotic state it was in, and could develop efficient and economic administration of the two services. The Board was constituted from a combination of:

(a) The public health branch of the Privy Council responsible for scientific and medical functions of the old Board of Health.

(b) The Local Government Act department of the Home Office which dealt with loans to local authorities and urban areas.

(c) The Poor Law Board.

Thus was established a single central authority with measurable powers over local authorities constituted by the Sanitary Authority provisions of the *Public Health Act*, 1875.

FINANCIAL DEVELOPMENT

8. Growing financial relationship. The *Poor Law Act*, 1834, and the *Municipal Corporations Act*, 1835, made no provision for central government aid. It became apparent however that involvement by the government in the welfare of the community must involve taxation and the transference of resources among various groups of the community.

By 1888 the matter of central government grants-in-aid to local authorities had become sufficiently important for a review of the basis of financial relationships between local and central government, and to warrant an attempt to establish an independent source of finance for local authorities. The system of Assigned Revenues introduced after 1888 (by Goschen) failed, and its failure led to the recognition that local authorities could only work effectively if in partnership with the central government.

9. Rates versus grants. As the burden of expenditure increased upon the local authorities as a result of the growing social legislation, culminating in the great Liberal government reforms of 1907–1909, the demand for aid from central funds grew.

A tendency developed for the central government to undertake financial responsibility for certain services: *e.g.* the cost of criminal prosecutions; the cost of certain medical services. The grant-in-aid became to be used for a dual purpose:

(a) To relieve the burden on agricultural rate payers.
(b) Of extreme importance, *to improve administration standards.*

10. The House of Lords Committee, 1851. In considering the financial relationships involved in the performance of a service, the committee laid down the following principle: "whenever any new expenditure is proposed, the presumption is to be in favour of making it a national charge, and an exception should only be made . . . on account of special circumstances." Such circumstances could be "the expediency of the service being on a local basis, or the continued usage and connection of the particular institution with the habits and usage of the county."

The importance of the future system to be followed was illustrated by the early grants for police and highways: *e.g.* the *Police (Counties and Boroughs) Act,* 1856, allowed a grant of one-quarter towards the cost of clothing and the pay of local forces, provided they *were certified by Home Office inspectors to be efficient* in numbers and discipline.

CENTRAL CONTROL FROM 1888

11. Main features. Three important features influenced the growth of central control during this period:

(a) *Administrative science.* The science of administration developed and enabled the old problems of lack of knowledge of local conditions and lack of effective control to be overcome by the central government.

(b) *End of laissez-faire.* The effective ending of *laissez-faire* contributed to the increasing involvement of the government in all spheres of national life.

(c) *Financial dependence.* Local authorities became increasingly dependent on financial aid from the central government, with a consequent loss of independence.

12. Central departments. The Poor Law Commission and Board had suffered by their general inability to issue orders unless these were communicated to the Home Secretary and laid before Parliament for 40 days, during which they could be annulled.

NOTE: An important development under the Poor Law system was the growth of the *inspectorial system* with its diffusing of knowledge, anticipating the modern "informal control" methods.

The Local Government Board was more powerful in that, after acquiring the status of a ministry in 1879, it gradually acquired complete financial responsibility for all local government, with the exemption of the basic functions of the municipal corporations. This financial control heralded the control of policy.

13. Effects of the war. The First World War highlighted the weakness of the Local Government Board, namely its lack of unified policy; its lack of compulsory powers; and its division of responsibilities. The War thus showed the need for one central authority with clear responsibility for all the functions classifiable under "public health." In 1919 the *Ministry of Health* was established with full executive powers.

14. Financial development. The Departmental Committee on Local Taxation established a presumptive case for increased grants-in-aid, and increased central intervention was justified on the following grounds:

   (a) The inadequacy of local revenues.
   (b) The correction of inequalities.
   (c) The maintenance of national standards in the public interest.

The distinction between national and local services appropriate to a pre-industrial society could no longer be maintained in the light of the nineteenth and twentieth century developments, and the community took on the aspect of *a single community*. Central financial aid increased to fulfil the above-mentioned needs.

15. Subsequent developments. Central government control is being emphasised by a general tendency to concentrate all the major powers in the hands of the central authority, and the imposition of central influence upon all aspects of local authority operations. There has been a general increase in the number and sophistication of methods of control, particularly since 1945, but always falling short of concentrating all control in a single department.

Legislation since 1940 has emphasised *the national importance of local services* and charged appropriate ministers with the duty of co-ordinating services and of achieving national standards.

FORMS OF ADMINISTRATIVE CONTROL

16. General features. These may broadly be classified into general powers of control and specific statutory powers of control, both together representing *formal* control, and the *informal* control through the pressures of advice and consultation.

17. Informal control. Considerable methods of control exist outside the statutory field, and are exercised through various conventional forms. Central government departments exercise advisory power in three main ways:

   (a) *Issue of circulars.* These consist of circular letters drawing attention to desirable and recommended procedures, and include practice codes, memoranda, etc. designed to raise the level of efficiency and to explain ministerial policy.

(b) *Answering problems.* The central ministries are often asked for guidance by local authorities, and exercise such guidance by replies to specific questions and the making of suggestions. The ministry in fact acts as a "clearing-house" for the dissemination of information.

(c) *Advice.* Informal advice to individual authorities through the inspectorial system.

NOTE: Informal control does not rest on any specific statutory authority but relies upon advice amounting in practice to administrative instruction. During a recent financial crisis, circulars advised local authorities in considering their budgets for 1958 and 1959 to aim at achieving all possible economies.

18. Why is informal control effective? The acceptance of non-mandatory control by local authority rests on several factors:

(a) *Partnership.* The relationship between local and central government, with consequent functional overlapping, involves the need to develop a form of partnership with a practical approach to their respective rights and duties.

(b) *Informal consultations.* The use of informal consultations prior to legislative changes, or to the imposition of new duties on local authorities, tightens the relationship between central and local authorities and enables standards to be set which are clarified by ministerial advice.

(c) *Sharing of knowledge.* Administrative and technical knowledge acquired by the central departments is made available for use by local authorities.

(d) *Conformity.* The background of central control is the necessity of ensuring conformity with standards set by the central authority, particularly where the central authority has at its disposal financial sanctions. Thus the local authorities are obliged to conform with ministerial policy upon which financial aid may depend, as suggested by the various pressures of informal control.

(e) *Ultimate sanction.* There always exists the ultimate sanction that the central authority may acquire statutory powers of compulsion, if local authorities do not conform to its informal rulings.

STATUTORY POWERS OF CONTROL

19. Meaning. Certain statutes conferring powers on central departments appear to vest in them considerable controlling powers over local authorities, although not granting absolute control: *e.g.* the *Education Act*, 1944 (*s.* 1), gives the Secretary of State for Education the duty "to promote the education of the people in England and Wales . . . and to secure the effective execution, by local authorities, under his control and direction, of the national policy for providing . . . educational services in every area." The Ministry however does not interpret the Act as giving overriding power, and control is generally achieved through specific sections: *e.g.* Section 68 gives the Minister power to issue directions in certain cases. Similar powers are conferred on the appropriate departments by the *Water Resources Act*, 1963, and the *Children Act*, 1948.

NOTE: In the field of education the introduction of the comprehensive system is proceeding by co-operation and not by the imposition of control.

20. Financial control. The increased financial contributions of the central government to local authorities has resulted in rigorous control, not only limited to individual services, but covering the whole role of local authorities in the national economy. This is described in **21–23** below.

21. Control over loans. By virtue of the *Local Government Act*, 1933 (s. 195), a local authority may, *with the consent of the Minister*, borrow money for the execution of permanent works, such as the purchase of land and the erection of buildings, the cost of which in the opinion of the Minister ought to be spread over a term of years. The sanctioning minister is the Minister of Housing and Local Government, or where appropriate the Minister of Transport, subject to consultation with other interested departments, *e.g.* education. Local authorities are usually forced to borrow for all major capital projects because these cannot be financed from the rates, and the view is held that such expenditure, being for the benefit of posterity, should not fall on the shoulders of a single generation of ratepayers.

The local authorities' need to borrow means a considerable measure of control in the hands of the central government, as it would be impossible to start a new service or to expand an existing one without recourse to borrowing.

The power of the Minister extends beyond the mere testing of the technical soundness of the proposed project, and involves an inquiry into the financial standing of the authority and the necessity of the scheme. The control enables the central authority to impose its will as regards the nature of the local authority's expansion, and it is of importance in time of national economic stringency when the rationing of capital is applied.

22. Control through grants. The increased and rapidly increasing contribution of the central government through grants-in-aid of local authorities has involved a corresponding increase in the powers of control and the influence it exercises over local authorities.

(a) *General grants.* Detailed control is not a feature of such grants, but the Minister has the power to reduce such a grant if satisfied that an authority has failed to achieve or to maintain reasonable standards in the provision of certain services. However, such a decision may not be made arbitrarily and must be approved by the House of Commons after a ministerial report has been considered. (In the same way ministerial standards must be approved beforehand by the House.) A similar power exists under the *Housing (Financial Provisions) Act*, 1958, in cases where an authority fails to discharge any of its duties under the Housing Acts, or any condition subject to which central government contribution is made.

The procedure for reducing general grants is rather cumbersome and the force of this form of control lies in the threat of reduction rather than applications of the power, and this will generally be enough to ensure the maintenance of standards.

(b) *Specific grants.* A more potent form of financial control exists in the field of specific grants, and the notion of "approved" expenditure. Detailed control over expenditure and efficiency is a feature of specific grants, and, as the central government will often only pay grants where standards are approved by the ministries, this has the effect of making local authorities follow ministerial policy rather than use their discretion.

23. Examples of grants. Section 4, *Housing Act*, 1961, requires the Minister of Housing and Local Government to pay a contribution to any local authority towards houses which he approves built by that authority. His approval depends on matters such as need, standards of construction, design and amenity. The Minister's view is not subject to appeal, and the effect of such control is to enable the imposition of ministerial policy standards on local authorities, although this is modified by reasonable application by the Ministry and by prior consultation with the authorities as to the required standards.

A similar power is granted to the Home Secretary over the police under the *Police Act*, 1964, which makes payment of a grant conditional on the Home Secretary's being satisfied as to such matters as efficiency, staffing, rates of pay, conditions of service and co-operation with other forces. If he is not satisfied, the grant may be reduced or withheld.

24. Inspection. Closely allied to control through grants is the long-established inspectorial system. Inspectors are often used to impress upon and inform local authorities of ministerial policy and standards. Although the practice mainly operates only in the education, police and fire services, its importance must not be underestimated nor must it be regarded purely as a form of "checking." The importance of the inspectorate is that it exerts influence not by the issue of orders, but by providing for the interchange of ideas, for the pooling of experience, and for a direct link between the central department and the local authority. In particular inspectors are disseminators of technical knowledge and developments.

25. Approval of schemes. A wide range of central government control is carried on through the comparatively modern system of approval of schemes. In spite of its recent origins, this is proving one of the fastest developing and most effective forms of control. The technique is to require local authorities to submit schemes for carrying out certain services, after the basic principles have been laid down in the enabling statute.

The system may be justified on the following grounds:

(*a*) *Local variations.* Variations in size of population, area, and of resources between local authorities makes it difficult to establish one overall statutory scheme appropriate for all authorities.

(*b*) *Devolution.* Excessive concentration of work at the centre in minutely detailing all legislative enactments would mean the breakdown of the legislative system.

(*c*) *Local initiative.* It enables local authorities to fulfil their responsibility and exercise initiative on behalf of their area, whilst retaining overall control at the centre.

26. Examples of schemes. Under the *Education Act*, 1944, each local authority has a duty to determine the actual and

D

future needs in its area, and must submit to the Secretary of State a plan showing the action which the authority proposes to take to fulfil those needs. Similar procedures exist under the *National Health Service Act*, 1946, and the *National Assistance Act*, 1948, for carrying out duties under those Acts.

Town and Country Planning Act, 1962. Under *s*. 4 each local planning authority is required to survey its area and submit to the Minister its proposals for determining the use of land in the area, and the stages by which the proposed development is to be carried out. The Minister is empowered to prescribe the form and content of the plan which is required by statute to deal with certain matters, *e.g.* allocation for industrial, agricultural and residential use. The Minister may vary the plan submitted in detail, or may make alterations which destroy the whole underlying concept of the plan. Thus the plan which is at the basis of local planning control is to a large extent subject to the requirements of central policy, and the work of the local planning authority becomes mainly administrative.

27. Conclusions on the method. The above form of control is particularly effective in that, while leaving local authorities with a measure of discretionary power, it enables the central authority to discharge its responsibilities to maintain standards and avoid extravagance. This control may be increased by the preparation of model schemes by the central authority and by the consultation which takes place before a final plan is submitted. It enables the central authority to impose its will and policy on local authorities by virtue of its power to reject or amend schemes *which do not comply with ministerial policy*.

28. Control over officers. In certain comparatively limited cases the law gives a minister some degree of control over the appointment, remuneration or dismissal of local government officers:

(*a*) *Clerk to the council*. The salary of the clerk must be approved.

(*b*) *County medical officer of health*. In this case qualifications are laid down by the Minister, and in cases where grant aid is in operation consent is needed for dismissal (so also for *Public Health Inspectors*).

(*c*) *Education*. The local education authorities may, under the *Education Act*, 1944, only appoint a chief education officer after consultation with and approval by the Minister.

This intervention causes resentment by the local authorities, and is regarded as an unnecessary and unwarranted interference in local affairs.

29. Regulations. Certain statutes conferring powers or duties on local authorities expressly give the minister concerned the power of making regulations. Generally the statute will outline the main provisions about a service, and will enable the minister to make the necessary provisions for putting the service into effect. This increases ministerial power, particularly as Parliament has rarely the time or inclination to check on the efficient use of such regulations.

30. Powers in default. In certain cases where local authorities fail to carry out their statutory responsibilities, a minister is empowered to issue directions or to transfer the functions to another local authority or to himself.

The principal examples of such a power are found under the *Public Health Act*, 1936, and the *Education Act*, 1944. The powers are rarely if ever used, as disputes involved are likely to be resolved by other means before reaching this final level. However, they exist and exercise a salutory effect on local authorities.

31. Confirmation of bye-laws. Bye-laws made by a local authority must be submitted to the central departments concerned for confirmation, and in many cases must comply with the model systems issued centrally.

32. Issue of directions. These are greatly limited in scope, and any extension is strongly opposed as it would tend to destroy the last vestiges of local autonomy. The principal examples are:

   (*a*) *In planning* the Minister may require certain types of planning application to be referred to him for decision.
   (*b*) Issue of directions to authorities in default.

33. Hearing of appeals. The Minister will be required to exercise a judicial role in the following cases:

   (*a*) Disputes between authorities.

(b) Disputes between local authorities and officers.
(c) Disputes between local authorities and private individuals, *e.g.* planning appeals or disputes about compulsory purchase.

34. Consent to individual acts. In limited cases the Minister's consent is required before a local authority can act, *e.g.* sales of council houses.

35. District audit. (*See* IX, 53.) It is doubted whether this can strictly be described as central control, since the auditors, although civil servants, are in fact required to exercise an independent judicial function based upon the application of legal, and not administrative, standards.

CONCLUSIONS

36. Cumulative effect. The multitude of powers of varying degrees of importance which the central departments exercise over local authorities must be viewed not as isolated instances but as a total influence. The whole effect is one which, while enabling local authorities to exercise a certain degree of local autonomy, does force them to comply with the policy standards of the central government. Central control falls short of complete dictatorship over local authorities, but the underlying tone of the powers of control is that of bending the local authorities to the will of the central government.

As a result local authorities tend to resort to the centre for guidance even when this is not legally or practically required. The first reaction of a local authority is often to turn to the regional office of the appropriate Ministry for advice, and whenever an authority seeks to clarify its legal position its first move is to consider the role of the Minister. Thus this dependent attitude and the wide powers of "influence" and control tend to make local authorities act as local administrative bodies responsible for considering local variations, but basically responsible for applying central policy.

37. Justification of central control.

(a) *Role of the state.* The role of the state in the affairs of the nation has greatly increased. It now consists of a series of functions for providing beneficial services for the welfare of each citizen, and for promoting national economic prosperity.

(b) *Defects of local authorities.* Local authorities through their variations of area, population and resources are incapable of providing a uniformity of service throughout the country, and so responsibility for this must rest with the central government. In particular the basic fault of the rating system is that resources are least adequate where they are most needed.

(c) *Financial assistance.* Local authorities are financially dependent on the central government, and are becoming increasingly more so. With financial aid from the centre is coupled increasing control over the expenditure of local authorities. The state, therefore, as holder of the purse strings, has a responsibility to the taxpayer.

(d) *Uniformity.* The responsibility of the state is for securing uniform development and the establishment of national minima, and this can only be achieved through close control.

(e) *Greater resources.* The central government has greater resources than local authorities, and has a greater pool of skilled administrative and technical staff.

(f) *National interests.* "The interests of the local areas must be subservient to the interests of the nation as a whole, and so there must be control from the centre to achieve the dominance of this interest" (*Bentham*).

38. Disadvantages of central control. It must be accepted that some degree of central control is inevitable and desirable in the context of modern social and economic conditions. However, certain disadvantages stem from an excess of such control.

(a) *Local variations.* By its sheer size and remoteness from the local scene of operations, the central authority is unable to take proper account of local differences in need and operating conditions.

(b) *Local initiative.* The weight of central control and the enforcement of central policy is destroying local initiative.

(c) *Loss of interest.* The extremely poor response of voters in local elections, far below the interest displayed in foreign systems which are less dominated by the state, may be attributed to a large extent to the lack of local power. It also contributes to the poorer class of councillor and employee, as persons of ability are less likely to be attracted owing to the lack of discretion granted to them.

NOTE: The Local Government Manpower Committee in 1949 suggested that the relationship should be based on the premise that "local authorities are responsible bodies competent to discharge their own functions and that . . . they exercise their responsibilities in their own right . . . the objective (of central control) should be to leave as much as possible of the detailed management of a scheme or service to the local authority and to concentrate the department's control at key points where it can most effectively discharge its responsibilities for government policy and financial administration."

39. Areas of local independence. The following, which are dealt with more fully in other parts of the book, may be regarded as areas where local authorities have a degree of discretion:

(a) Internal organisation.
(b) Employment of staffs.
(c) Income from rates.
(d) Suggesting alterations.

It is thought, however, that these pale into insignificance beside the colossus of central control. It should also be observed that local authorities are able to exert "pressure group" power through their various associations, *e.g.* the County Councils Association, and as a collective body are able to require prior consultation and consideration when the government proposes any legislative changes.

40. The Maud Committee. The following recommendations of the Maud Committee on the relations between local and central government contain important reform proposals, and must be considered in the light of their possible future mandatory application.

(a) *Discretion.* There is a need to check the steady reduction of the discretion allowed to local authorities, and their conversion into mere agencies of the central government.

(b) *Internal powers.* They must be allowed to determine their own internal organisation.

(c) *Officers.* Whitehall should play no part in the appointment and dismissal of chief officers.

(d) *Allowances.* Local authorities should be allowed to determine individually the rate of financial allowances to members.

(e) *Investment policy.* In the national interest Whitehall should control local investment, but not to the extent of controlling details of local building or expenditure.

(f) *Co-ordination.* Central departments must co-ordinate

among themselves their dealings with local authorities, so that the authorities may establish their own priorities as part of a co-ordinated plan for development.

(*g*) *Simplification.* There is a need for revision, reduction, and simplification of the complexity of central administrative control.

(*h*) *Local finance.* The taxing powers of local authorities must be strengthened and dependence on central finances reduced, and a greater realism on loan sanction developed.

(*i*) *General competence powers.* Local authorities should be given general competence powers (as in Sweden) to do whatever in their opinion is in the interests of their area and inhabitants, subject to their not encroaching on the duties of other government bodies, and to appropriate safeguards for the protection of public and private interests.

41. Summing-up. It is however suggested that, despite any recommendations which any committee may make, the only true hope of local independence lies ultimately in the reorganisation of local authorities on a larger and more powerful basis (*see* XII).

PROGRESS TEST 7

1. What are the characteristics of central government control as practised in England and Wales?   (**1–3**)

2. Outline the early development of central control.   (**4–7**)

3. Outline the financial aspects involved in this development. (**8–10**)

4. What were the principal features of central control in the period 1888–1929?   (**11–14**)

5. Outline in general terms the trends after 1929.   (**15**)

6. What is meant by and involved in informal administrative control, and why is it effective?   (**17, 18**)

7. What general statutory powers of control exist?   (**19**)

8. Describe the main methods of financial control.   (**20–23**)

9. What other important forms of central control exist?   (**24–35**)

10. What is the cumulative effect of central control?   (**36**)

11. How may such control be justified?   (**37**)

12. What are the principal disadvantages of central control? (**38**)

13. To what extent do local authorities still enjoy any independence?   (**39**)

14. What recommendations did the Maud Committee make about central control?   (**40**)

CHAPTER VIII

THE LEGAL STATUS OF LOCAL AUTHORITIES

THE CORPORATE STATUS

1. Local authorities as corporations. The one characteristic feature of local authorities in England and Wales is that they all have corporate status, with the consequent rights and obligations which flow from this.

The principal feature of *corporate status* is that it vests the group of individuals acquiring it with a collective entity existing independently of the persons who comprise it. Upon incorporation the collection of individuals becomes a single body, or legal *persona* having rights and duties, capable of holding and disposing of property, and of bringing and defending actions at law, quite independently of the rights and duties of any of its members. Other characteristics of a corporation are:

(a) *Name*. A corporation must have a name and must enter into all transactions under that name.

(b) *Perpetual succession*. A corporation has perpetual succession and therefore continues to exist independently of its members. The mere fact that the membership of a local authority changes following an election has no legal effect on the legal position of the authority itself, and thus obligations entered into on behalf of the authority by past members continue to bind it.

(c) *Seal*. A corporation has a seal, and as a general rule its acts will be authenticated by the fixing of the seal. (But see the effect of the *Corporate Bodies Contracts Act*, 1960.)

2. Modes of incorporation. At the present time incorporation will be effected by Royal Charter or by statute. Charter corporations are boroughs, whereas the Greater London Council, the London boroughs, county and district councils, and parish councils are statutory corporations. In the case of boroughs, the corporation may only act in the corporate name by the council acting on behalf of the corporation; the council is thus regarded as the sole agent of the corporation. In the case of statutory corporations the council is to be regarded as the body corporate.

THE DOCTRINE OF ULTRA VIRES

3. Meaning of the doctrine. Every corporation created by statute, whether it be a trading corporation, local authority, commercial corporation, or a public corporation, is legally entitled only to carry out acts for which there exists statutory authority. (In the case of commercial corporations the authority is contained in the objects clause of its articles of association.)

Whereas a natural person is legally entitled to carry out any act which the law does not forbid, a corporation may only carry out those acts which it is authorised to do. If an action is performed for which there is not statutory authority such an action will be *ultra vires* (beyond the powers) of the corporation, and void. The objects which a corporation may legally pursue, and the means of attaining these objects, must be "either expressly conferred or derived by reasonable implication from the provisions of a statute" (*Baroness Wenlock* v. *River Dee Corp. (1885)*).

4. Practical extension. It has been found that rigid application of the doctrine would have the effect of hampering local authorities, or of requiring very detailed legislation. In consequence a local authority has been judicially held to be entitled to do whatever is *reasonably incidental* to the carrying out of the express or implied powers.

5. Examples of the doctrine in practice. The following are illustrative of the practical application of, and judicial attitudes towards, the doctrine.

(a) *A.-G.* v. *Fulham Corporation.* A local authority was empowered under the *Baths and Washhouse Acts* of 1864 and 1878 to provide washing facilities where residents could wash their own clothes. In 1920 the authority introduced a scheme whereby residents could leave their washing to be laundered by council servants, and a collection and delivery service was arranged. An action was brought on behalf of a ratepayer by the Attorney-General for a *declaration* that the action of the authority was illegal. HELD: The scheme was *ultra vires*, as the

Act contained no express or implied powers for the provision of a washing service as opposed to the mere provision of facilities for use by the residents.

(b) *Roberts* v. *Hopwood* (1925). Under the *Metropolis Management Act*, 1855, local authorities were empowered to pay their employees such wages *as they thought fit*. The council resolved to pay a higher wage than that obtaining in other parts of the country in order to establish itself as a "model employer." The district auditor disallowed the excess wages and surcharged those responsible for their authorisation. HELD: If expenditure upon a lawful object is excessive it will be unreasonable and therefore *ultra vires*.

NOTE: The courts obviously take the view that Parliament cannot be taken to authorise anything unreasonable.

6. Effects of ultra vires acts.

(a) An *ultra vires* contract is void *ab initio*.

(b) Where such an act has been authorised by members of the council, and its execution has thus resulted in illegal expenditure of public funds, such persons may be surcharged by the district auditor and ordered to repay the funds.

7. Does the doctrine apply to boroughs? There is a certain amount of contention about whether charter corporations are subject to the doctrine of *ultra vires*. The controversy stems from the status of boroughs as common law corporations, which were substantially in the same position as ordinary individuals, and subject only to the limitations imposed in their charters—which in practice was not a formidable deterrent to complete freedom of action.

The *Municipal Corporations Act*, 1882, as interpreted by the House of Lords in *Tynemouth Corporation* v. *A.G.* (1899) seemed to establish the rule that charter corporations were subject to the doctrine. However, the *Local Government Acts*, 1933 and 1958, adopted different wording from the 1882 Act. The High Court in *A.G.* v. *Leicester Corporation* following the wording of the 1933 Act held that chartered boroughs were not subject to the doctrine.

8. Situation in practice. Though the point is not settled, the following factors seem to point to the view that local authorities are subject to the doctrine, irrespective of whether or not they are created by statute:

(a) *Practice.* In practice, when challenged on the ground of *ultra vires*, chartered authorities do not seek to defend such actions by reliance on their status as common law corporations, but seek other grounds of defence.

(b) *Legislative intervention.* With the close control the central government exercises over local authorities, any attempt freely to dissipate funds would soon result in legislative or other sanctions being applied.

(c) *Doubt as to High Court decision.* It is generally felt that the decision in the *Leicester* case is of doubtful value, owing to its conflicting with the House of Lords decision in the *Tynemouth* case.

(d) *The prerogative.* Charter corporations are created by exercise of the prerogative. The prerogative is subordinate in fields covered by statute. As a large sphere of local government activity is prescribed by statute, the area left free to local authorities would in any case be extremely limited.

9. Remedies against ultra vires actions. Two possible forms of remedy exist where an action of a local authority is complained of as being *ultra vires*:

(a) *High Court action.* An action may be brought for a declaration or for a declaration coupled with an injunction (*see* **22** below).

(b) *District audit.* The alleged *ultra vires* expenditure can be brought to the attention of the district auditor, who may then surcharge the persons responsible (*see* **5** above).

NOTE: Certain recent Acts have authorised local authorities to spend a limited amount on matters for which they have no statutory authority. In addition the Maud Committee has recommended the abolition of the doctrine and its replacement by "general competence" powers, which would enable local authorities to act in the interests of its citizens as it thought fit, subject to certain safeguards.

BYE-LAWS

10. Power to make bye-laws.

(a) *Definition.* A law, made under the auspices of a statutory grant of power, enabling local authorities to make laws having force for the area of their authority. Unlike Parliament the legislative powers of local authorities must stem from statute, but when exercised validly the bye-laws created have the force of law in their area of operation.

(b) *Statutory powers.* Generally a local authority must show specific statutory power to justify a particular bye-law. However, county councils and county borough councils are granted, by the *Local Government Act,* 1933 (*s.* 249), the general power of making bye-laws for the "good rule and government of their area" and "for the suppression of nuisances." Although this provision enables the making of a wide range of bye-laws, an effective check is provided by:

(*i*) The need to obtain ministerial approval.

(*ii*) The need to satisfy judicial tests as to validity of bye-laws.

11. Ministerial consent. When a bye-law is made, but before it takes effect, it must be submitted to an appropriate confirming authority. This is generally the Home Secretary, but it may be the Minister of Housing and Local Government where matters of public health are involved.

The confirming authority will examine the bye-law from the following viewpoints:

(*a*) Necessity.

(*b*) Whether it is *ultra vires.*

(*c*) Whether it is likely to satisfy the judicial tests as to validity.

12. Judicial tests as to validity. Whereas the only jurisdiction a court has over a parliamentary statute is that of interpretation, bye-laws have to satisfy the long-established tests as to validity:

(*a*) *Reasonableness.* A bye-law will not be enforced unless it is reasonable in the sense that it must not discriminate unfairly, be made in bad faith, or amount to unreasonable or oppressive intervention.

(*b*) *Certainty.* A bye-law will not be upheld unless "it contains adequate information as to the duties of those who are to obey and is certain in terms" (*Kruse* v. *Johnson* (1904)). Thus if the bye-law is ambiguous in its terms it will not be enforced.

(*c*) *It must be consistent with the general law.* A bye-law which attempts to prohibit what the general law expressly or impliedly permits, or attempts to legalise what the law prohibits, will be void. It will also be void if repugnant to the general principles of the common law.

(*d*) It must be *intra vires.*

LIABILITY IN CONTRACT, TORT AND CRIME

13. Contractual liability.

(a) *Formal requirements.* The *Local Government Act*, 1933, stipulates that local authorities on entering into contracts shall comply with the standing orders of the council. In particular, contracts for the supply of goods, the execution of works, and the supply of materials must be regulated in standing orders as to the publication, etc. of the invitation to tender.

(b) *Disclosure of interest: see* V, **17**(b).

(c) *Sealing of contracts.* Up to 1960 a local authority was required to enter into all contracts under seal, with the exception of contracts involving trifling sums and contracts for recurring items. Under the *Corporate Bodies Contracts Act*, 1960, the following rules now govern the making of contracts by local authorities.

(i) If the contract is one which, in the case of private individuals, is required to be entered into in writing or evidenced in writing, then it may be made by the authority in writing.

(ii) If the contract is one which may be entered into by an individual orally it may be so entered into by a local authority.

(d) *Who may contract?* Basically the normal rules as to agency apply in the case of contracts entered into on behalf of a local authority by its employees. In particular an officer has authority to enter into all contracts covering matters incidental to his main contracting purposes; and if a person has good reason to believe that an officer or servant of the authority has power to contract on its behalf, the authority may be liable notwithstanding the express power to contract not having been conferred on the authority or servant.

14. Tortious liability of servants.

Local authorities can be liable in tort even though the action complained of as being tortious is *ultra vires*. However, any liability in tort must of necessity be committed through the acts of the authority's servants, etc., and therefore the authority's liability being *vicarious* the following classes must be considered.

(a) *Servants.* A servant is defined as a "person subject to the direction of his employer as to the manner in which he shall carry out his work." A local authority is liable for the torts of its servants in accordance with the usual law of master and servant. Consequently any tort committed by a servant in the "*course of his employment*" renders the authority liable. In this way local authorities have been held liable for a variety of torts, including defamation and false imprisonment.

(*b*) *Professional servants.* Although a professional servant of a local authority is not strictly under the direction of the local authority as to the way in which he carries out his work, it has been judicially held that this does not affect the liability of the local authority. It was pointed out in *Cassidy* v. *Minister of Health* (1951) that the key factor was that the authority was liable because it had the ultimate sanction of dismissal over the servant.

(*c*) *Independent statutory duties.* If the servant has independent statutory duties vested in him by virtue of his office, the local authority will not be liable for his torts merely because they employ him: *e.g.* where the employee commits a tort in the course of carrying out duties imposed upon him by a government department.

15. Tortious liability of contractors and agents.

(*a*) *Independent contractors.* These are defined as persons "engaged to carry out a particular piece of work, etc. over which the council exercises no control, its responsibility being limited to satisfying itself that the work conforms to the terms of the contract," *e.g.* builders employed by the council.

In *principle* the authority is not liable for torts committed by such persons with certain *exceptions*:

(*i*) Where the authority interferes to prescribe how the work shall be carried out.

(*ii*) Where the authority specifically authorises the tortious act.

(*iii*) Where the work carried out is particularly dangerous.

(*iv*) Where the independent contractor is carrying out a statutory duty of the local authority.

(*b*) *Agents.* In this case the extent and nature of the authority's liability will depend on the extent and degree of the authority's control over the agent.

16. Statutory authority. The plea of statutory authority is a valid defence in proceedings for nuisance or trespass, provided the authority can show that it was under a statutory *duty* to act in the way it did. Where the method of acting is permissive or discretionary, the authority is not empowered to commit torts in carrying out the acts. Also when the authority is performing a duty, it will be liable for acts of *negligence* committed in the course of performing the duty.

17. Breach of statutory duty. Where damage has been caused as the result of a local authority failing to carry out a statutory duty, liability will only be established if the plaintiff is able to prove the following:

(a) *Duty not power*. The duty must be absolute and not be a mere discretionary power to act.

(b) *Absence of statutory remedy*. If the relevant statute contains a remedy this will generally exclude any claim for damages, unless the court treats the construction of the statute as not excluding the common law remedy.

(c) *Duty to the individual*. The plaintiff must show that the duty was owed to a particular class of the public, of which he is one.

18. Criminal liability. A corporate body may be convicted of a criminal offence, except those only punishable by imprisonment.

19. Personal liability.

(a) *Members*. Corporate status will generally preclude the individual liability of members, but where the action is *ultra vires* such members may be surcharged by the district auditor.

(b) *Servants*. In the case of torts committed by servants, the plaintiff may sue either the servant or the authority. However, certain statutory provisions exempt servants from personal liability: *e.g.* under the *Highways Act*, 1959 (*s.* 261), members and servants are protected from liability in carrying out the Act, provided they act *bona fides*.

JUDICIAL CONTROL OF LOCAL AUTHORITIES

20. General background. Judicial control is defined as the special procedure for control exercised by the High Court, as opposed to the determination of liability in the above cases. The absence of special administrative courts in the United Kingdom, such as those that exist in France, raises the question as to whether adequate remedies against local government exist. However, despite the absence of special courts, there are two basic presumptions which form the basis of control of the rights of the individual citizen against local government.

(a) The local authorities are in the main successors to the justices of the peace, and thus become subject to special forms of control exercised by the Queen's Bench Division of the High Court.

(b) Local authorities, as a result of their corporate status, are legal persons, and thus liable to the same remedies as those available against private individuals.

21. Special remedies. One must therefore consider "special" remedies and also remedies against private persons, bearing in mind that local authorities are not really ordinary persons, and have special rights, powers and duties conferred by statute. Thus the principal concern of the courts is not with ordinary wrongs, but with the improper use of specific rights and powers, and the failure to perform statutory duties.

22. Statutory appeals, etc. Before considering special remedies one may observe two cases of direct intervention by the courts.

(a) *Court approval.* In certain cases the consent of the appropriate court must be obtained before certain action may be taken by a local authority: *e.g.* a Nuisance Abatement Order must be obtained from a magistrates' court.

(b) *Appeals to court.* In certain cases appeals against the decisions of local authorities lie to the courts: *e.g.*

(i) To a *magistrates' court* against repair or demolition orders issued under the *Public Health Act, 1936.*

(ii) To the *High Court* against a compulsory purchase order.

In some instances the court's powers will be limited to merely applying the legal principles in any case, whereas in others the court may be empowered to substitute its discretion for that of the authority.

The High Court views its duty in such cases as being that of "keeping the balance between the local authority and the individuals [in this case the owners of defective buildings] . . . and the court whilst respecting the duties of the local authority must protect the owner from undue burdens" (*Denning L.J. in Cochrane* v. *Chanctonbury R.D.C.* (1950)).

23. Declarations and injunctions. The legality of an act or decision of a local authority may be determined by a High Court action for a declaration, or for a declaration coupled with an injunction.

An *injunction* issues to restrain the local authority from doing some act which it threatens to do or to repeat.

A *declaration* arises where the plaintiff merely asks the court to state what the law is, and this is usually adequate in a legal controversy with a local authority. A local authority will respect a declaration even though no sanction is involved, and in any case the courts action may be supported by suitable administrative, or even legislative, action.

The method is advocated by the courts as a means of controlling administrative bodies, and it is wider in scope than the prerogative orders, as it is not limited to the judicial or quasi-judicial functions of the local authority.

(a) *Who may sue?* Proceedings about the breach of public rights are theoretically brought by the Attorney-General, and a person wishing to institute such an action must obtain the Attorney-General's consent, who will then sue at the "relation of" the individual. A private individual may only bring a personal action if his private right is interfered with, or he has suffered some damage from the breach of a public right which is peculiar to himself.

(b) *Use of procedure.* The action is generally sought to challenge *ultra vires* acts or acts in breach of public rights.

24. The prerogative orders. These are special remedies available in the Queen's Bench Division of the High Court to control the wrongful exercise of jurisdiction by inferior bodies. It will not be issued "as of right" and the applicant must establish a *prima facie* case.

The orders assume three forms, as described in **25** and **26** below.

25. The order of mandamus. This is the ultimate means of compelling a public authority to carry out a statutory duty, and takes the form of a command from the High Court directing the authority to perform a duty which has been neglected. The remedy is discretionary and the following tests must be satisfied before it will be issued:

(a) *Absolute duty.* The duty must be absolute and not discretionary. The court cannot compel the exercise of a discretionary power, nor control the manner in which a discretion is exercised. It will however lie to compel the authority to exercise a discretion where it is under a statutory duty to do so.

(b) *Personal interest.* The applicant must show that he himself has a substantial personal interest in the performance of the duty.

(c) *Other remedies.* It will not be granted where an equally beneficial, convenient and effective remedy exists.

NOTE: The order has been issued to compel the holding of council elections, the levying of a rate and the appointment of aldermen. Disobedience will render a person guilty of contempt of court, and the court may order other persons to carry out the duty on behalf of the authority.

26. The orders of prohibition and certiorari. These orders issue according to the same principles and so they are considered together for convenience.

Prohibition issues to prevent the doing of an act. *Certiorari* lies to remove a case from one "court" to a higher court. In the local government sphere the usual remedy sought is *"certiorari to quash"* which will remove certain issues from an inferior tribunal, so that they may be reviewed by the High Court and if necessary quashed.

The term "court" is given an extended meaning and will cover every case where a public authority takes a decision affecting the rights of an individual in proceedings or circumstances which are judicial or "quasi-judicial" in nature. In *R.* v. *Local Government Board* (1882) it was stated that "wherever the legislature entrusts to any body, other than the superior courts, the power of imposing an obligation upon individuals, the court ought to exercise as widely as possible the power of controlling those bodies of persons if those persons admittedly attempt to exercise powers beyond those given to them by the law."

NOTE: The orders will only lie where the acts of the authority are judicial or quasi-judicial, as opposed to being of a mere administrative nature.

27. Use of the orders. The orders of prohibition and *certiorari* are used in the following cases:

(*a*) Control of *ultra vires*.

(*b*) Where an error of law is disclosed by the decision of a local authority in its reasons given for the decision.

(*c*) Where a local authority has employed incorrect procedure and has consequently prejudiced the rights of an individual.

(*d*) Where the rules of *natural justice* have not been observed: *i.e.* the decision-making body of the local authority has contained persons with an interest in the outcome of the decision, or where the local authority has denied the right to present a case either in writing, or orally. Note that this does not mean that normal legal procedure must be followed.

CONCLUSIONS

28. The defects of judicial control. Judicial control as a means of controlling local authorities suffers from the following defects:

(*a*) *Expense, etc.* A private individual must be prepared to undertake the trouble and expense of litigation, and as a result there must be some substantial personal interest of a financial or proprietary nature at stake to encourage the taking of legal action. This criticism of course does not apply in cases of actions between two local authorities.

(*b*) *Dilatory procedure.* The seeking of a remedy may involve long-drawn-out procedure: *e.g.* the seeking of an order *nisi*, the appearance to answer defence arguments, and possible further proceedings. In addition local authorities have very considerable resources and are able to fight an action to final appeal level.

(*c*) *Effects on administration.* A judicial decision may upset long-established procedure, and a need arises to compare the cost of the loss of rapid and effective administration with the advantages of judicial control.

(*d*) *Locus standi.* It is often difficult, owing to the conditions precedent attached to many of the forms of judicial control outlined above, for an individual to establish his right to bring an action. Thus even though a public right has been infringed, interested parties may find it difficult to institute proceedings, and the preoccupation of the courts with procedural detail will consequently act as a deterrent to bringing an action.

(*e*) The limitation of the writs of *certiorari* and prohibition by the concept of the "quasi-judicial" decision inhibits the use of the remedies.

(*f*) The courts are only able to control illegal administration as opposed to the much more common *maladministration*.

29. Judicial versus administrative control. Judicial control tends to compare unfavourably with administrative control. The latter has the following advantages not found in judicial control:

    (a) *Not haphazard.* Administrative control is not left to the haphazard actions of interested private individuals, but is administered by permanent, trained officials charged with putting it into effect.

    (b) *Efficiency.* Administrative control involves the division of responsibility for services among departments with more concentrated checking. It may prevent abuses by keeping authorities informed of administrative policy.

    (c) *Compulsion.* It has powers of compulsion not dependent on the commission of some specific injury.

    (d) *Expediency.* It enables expediency as opposed to strict legal checks to be taken into account.

30. Why use judicial control? Judicial control can be justified on two main and vitally important grounds:

    (a) It is impartial and not tied to policy.

    (b) It secures public confidence that bias and corruption are not present in the administration of public business, whereas suspicions of these must always be present where administrative control is involved.

PROGRESS TEST 8

1. What is meant by "corporate" status? **(1, 2)**

2. Explain the doctrine of *ultra vires*, giving examples of its practical application. **(5, 6)** Does it apply to boroughs? **(7, 8)**

3. What remedies lie in respect of an *ultra vires* act? **(9)**

4. Under what authority may a local council make bye-laws? **(10)**

5. What tests as to the validity of bye-laws are applied? **(11, 12)**

6. Outline the principles of the contractual liability of local authorities. **(13)**

7. To what extent are local authorities liable for torts? **(14, 15)**

8. When may an action be brought against a local authority for injury resulting from its breach of a statutory duty? **(17)**

9. Explain the rules relating to the personal liability of members and servants of a local authority. **(19)**

10. Why is there judicial control? **(20, 21)**

11. What are the principle methods of judicial control of local authorities?   (22–27)

12. What are the main defects of judicial control?   (28) Do you consider that it serves a useful purpose?   (30)

13. What are the advantages of administrative control compared with judicial control?   (29)

CHAPTER IX

LOCAL GOVERNMENT FINANCE

INTRODUCTION

1. General picture. In 1965 local government expenditure amounted to over £400 million and is now fast approaching the £500 million mark. Of the £400 million £1,400,000 was *capital expenditure* and the rest *current expenditure*. The principle sources of local authority revenue are local *rates*, central government *grants*, *borrowing*, and trading receipts (principally council house rents). An examination of the development of the two principal sources, rates and grants, reveals the steadily growing influence of grants, involving a corresponding growth of local authority dependence on central financial assistance. The implications of this are dealt with in VII (Central Government Control), but it is pertinent to remark here that any views on the autonomy of local authorities must be read in the light of this financial relationship.

NOTE: In 1923–24 the proportion of grants to rate income was 52 per cent. In 1933–34 the proportion was 82 per cent, a figure which gradually rose to 100 per cent in the late 1930s. In 1943–44 the amount was 112 per cent, this being approximately the current figure, despite the transfer of important functions to the central government. Therefore the *real* proportion is in fact considerably higher.

2. Capital and revenue expenditure. A basic distinction in local finance has to be drawn between capital expenditure, *i.e.* that which is incurred on some object of lasting value, and current (or revenue) expenditure, *i.e.* usually of a constantly recurring nature and producing no permanent assets, for instance, expenditure on teachers' salaries.

The distinction is important from the point of view of local authority borrowing and the spreading of the cost to be borne by posterity. Generally all important capital expenditure is met by borrowing, whereas revenue expenditure comes from the general revenues of an authority, *i.e.* rates, grants and charges.

106

3. The basic problem. Income from charges, grants, etc. is deducted from the total expenditure of an authority and the balance is met from the rates. The basic problem is that of preventing the rates becoming an undue burden while reducing dependence as far as possible on state assistance, in accordance with the reasoning that state aid is linked with state control. Rates are an independent source of income which the local authority may use at its discretion on lawful objects.

FINANCIAL PROCEDURE

4. The budget. The statutory requirement that county councils must have an *annual* budget and appoint a *finance committee* has become the normal practice of all local authorities.

The financial year runs from 1st April to 31st March. Each committee considers its estimates of proposed expenditure, and the following procedure is followed:

(*a*) Preparation of estimates is generally undertaken by departmental staff in consultation with the treasurer. The estimates must allow for expansion of the department, price levels, wage levels, population increases, etc.

(*b*) The chief officer then submits a memorandum for the committee to work on.

(*c*) The committee usually bows to professional expertise and accepts the estimates without much discussion.

(*d*) All estimates are submitted to the *finance committee*.

5. The finance committee. The committee does not take final decisions, and it is possible that final cuts in estimates will have to be fought out at council level. The committee is limited by the general bounds of council policy, but within this may require cuts, and must combat the dangers of departmentalism by resolving competing claims. It may for example recommend a general percentage reduction in all spending, or make recommendations about the financing of capital expenditure.

6. Presentation. Ultimately the finance committee must balance expenditure and income, and present to the council all its financial proposals embodied in a resolution as to the rate to be levied, accompanied by appropriate reports, memoranda and statistics. No central government approval of the budget is required.

7. Internal financial control. This is exercised by the council, the finance committee and the officers. In particular:

(*a*) No expenditure may be made unless authority is contained in an appropriate council or committee resolution.

(*b*) Payment of all sums to and from the council must be made through the treasurer.

8. Effect of the budget. The budget is not absolutely binding, and therefore the council remains responsible for the continuing financial affairs of the authority. In particular supplementary estimates may arise which will have to follow the same course as the original estimates.

GRANTS

9. Reasons for grants. Originally, during the nineteenth century, the grant system was merely a method of appeasing the agricultural interests by enabling some of the costs of local government to be met from national taxation. This was subsequently reinforced by the realisation that the nation as a whole was interested in the maintenance of certain standards, and that the grant system could be used to attain them, and as a measure of control to enforce them on local authorities.

10. Justification of the grant system. The following arguments may be advanced in favour of the system:

(*a*) *New services*. These having been set up by the state it is only reasonable that the state should contribute to the cost of running them.

(*b*) *Burden*. The introduction of new services and the extension of existing ones would, without state help, place an intolerable burden upon local finance from rates and increase the defects inherent in the rating system.

(*c*) *Social legislation*. With modern social legislation it is impossible and unrealistic to divide services between the national and the local ones, as in many cases essentially national services are administered on a local basis because of the convenience of doing so.

(*d*) *Social responsibility*. It is the social obligation of the state to set a national minimum standard in the provision of services, and grant aid achieves this objective.

(*e*) *Need for control*. The attaining of national minima requires control from the central government, and the grant system with its financial leverage provides a convenient and efficient method of achieving such control.

(*f*) *Equalisation.* By determining grants on bases allowing for such matters as local resources and local needs, the state is enabled to reduce disparities between areas.

(*g*) *De-rating.* The state is responsible for de-rating provisions, exemptions, etc. which diminish local revenue, and therefore must be expected to help meet such deficiencies.

(*h*) *Increasing costs.* The constantly increasing costs of developing services, *e.g.* education, health, old people's welfare, and child services, could not be borne by the rate system.

11. Arguments against the grant system. The following arguments may be advanced against the grant system:

(*a*) *Financial dependence.* The growth of financial dependence upon the central government has greatly diminished the autonomy of local authorities.

(*b*) *Control.* It provides the most potent form of control (particularly when linked with control of borrowing), and tends to reduce local authorities from deliberative bodies to mere administrative agencies.

(*c*) *Inequalities.* It is open to question whether it is really effective in ironing out inequalities.

12. Principles of the grant system. The White Paper of 1928 may be taken as indicative of the principles which should underlie a system of central government grants. The question is how far the present system meets these requirements. The White Paper stated that "A proper system of grants should:

(*a*) Recognise that a fair contribution should be made by the Exchequer towards the cost of local services.

(*b*) Ensure that local authorities have complete financial interest in their administration.

(*c*) Be adapted in its working to the needs of the areas.

(*d*) Permit the greatest freedom of local administration and initiative.

(*e*) Provide sufficient central advice and control to ensure the achievement of a reasonable standard of performance."

TYPES OF GRANTS

13. Specific grants. These are grants made towards the cost of particular services and may be of the following types:

(*a*) *Percentage grants.* The payment of a percentage of "approved expenditure."

(b) *Unit grants.* A fixed amount paid by the Exchequer in respect of a determinable unit, *e.g.* grant for approved dwellings.

(c) *Special formula grants.* None exist at present for specific services but they existed in education up to 1948.

(d) *Discretionary grants.* These are payable to such bodies as coast protection authorities at the discretion of the Minister.

14. General grants. These may be of the following types:

(a) *Assigned revenues.* The payment of some source of tax over to the general revenues of local authorities. These are now virtually non-existent.

(b) *Block grants.* Grants-in-aid of local authorities on a general basis usually assessed on a formula, taking account of local needs, resources, etc.

HISTORICAL DEVELOPMENT

15. Origins. A small-scale start was made in 1835 with a grant to cover half the cost of the administration of justice, plus in 1845 a grant to cover half of the cost of certain expenditure of Poor Law Unions.

The system gathered force during the period 1870–80, when grants for elementary education, public health, police, prisons, registration and highways were made.

16. Assigned revenues. An attempt was made by *Goschen* in 1888 to abolish grants and replace them with revenues additional to, and more flexible than, rates. The *Local Government Act*, 1888, assigned the proceeds of various licences to local authorities. However, the growth of the social services during the Liberal administration of 1908–9 made such revenues insufficient and resulted in the need for further grants, generally on a *percentage* basis. The assigned revenues were effectively abolished in 1929, and are of negligible importance at the present day.

NOTE: It has been suggested that the considerable revenue from road fund licences could be allocated to local authorities.

17. Percentage grants. From the latter part of the nineteenth century down to 1929 these have been the principal type of grants, and such services as education and the police have always been aided on a percentage basis. So have most of the social services. Examples in force during this period were grants of 25 per cent of the cost of fire services, 75 per cent of Class I roads and 60 per cent of Class II roads.

However, percentage grants were generally objected to on the following grounds:

(a) *Too detailed* a control was involved.
(b) Their *"tied"* nature proved inconvenient.
(c) They encouraged local authorities to *extravagance* in that the authorities ignored the overall cost of providing a service and concentrated only on the actual cost to themselves.
(d) *Expenditure was uncontrollable.*

The period 1918–28 was one of considerable political controversy about the increasing level of public expenditure and taxation, both local and central. On the local level the attacks centred on the percentage grant system. The *Committee on National Expenditure* (1922) described percentage grants as "a money-spending device, but not an economic system."

THE BLOCK GRANT

18. Why favoured. The block (or *general Exchequer* grant) became increasingly favoured in that it had the following points in its favour:

(a) Increased the discretionary power of local authorities.
(b) Made local authorities responsible for any extravagance.
(c) Encouraged economies.

19. The Local Government Act, 1929. The Act abolished assigned revenues, introduced agricultural de-rating, and abolished certain percentage grants which it replaced with a general Exchequer contribution.

The Act also laid down the following principles which, despite defects in the machinery of the Act itself, remain established principles for the relations between central and local government:

(a) A recognition that there is a large area of local finance to which the general grant is appropriate.
(b) The general grant provides a way of dealing with the primary problem of disparity of financial resources between authorities.

The Act introduced the *block grant* assessed on a formula taking account of population, children under five, rateable value per head of population, proportion of unemployed in the area to the total population, and the sparsity of population. The grant was paid to county councils, with capitation payments to the districts, rural districts receiving one-fifth of the level for urban districts. The *percentage* grants remaining were principally those for police, education, roads and certain specified health services.

20. Defects of the Act. The following criticisms may be made:

    (a) The grant lagged behind expenditure, it being assessed on the previous year's expenditure.
    (b) De-rating severely reduced resources, which were not adequately covered by the grant.
    (c) It failed to attach enough importance to the levels of rateable value in various areas.

21. The Local Government Act, 1948. The transfer of functions to the central government that culminated in 1948, partly owing to the *Beveridge Report on the Social Services*, led to the need for recasting the central and local financial relationships. The Act of 1948 therefore:

    (a) *Introduced percentage grants* for children, health and fire services.
    (b) *Introduced a new block grant, i.e.* the Exchequer equalisation grant.

22. The Exchequer equalisation grant. This grant replaced the existing block grant and was designed to introduce a measure of equality into the financial resources of local authorities. The *weighted population* notion was retained, but on a formula calculated to help the poorer areas and to bring all authorities up to a minimum standard of rateable value per head.

The grant operated as follows: it made the Treasury act as a "ratepayer" for the amount needed in a particular area to cover any deficiency of rateable value per head as compared with the average for the country. In order to meet the criticism of the former block grant (that it lagged behind increases in local expenditure), it was provided that the grant was to be reviewed annually, and on the data available for the current year.

An important feature of the grant was its acceptance of the idea that not every authority was automatically entitled to a grant, and that, where the rateable value of an authority was above average, no grant was necessary.

23. Criticisms of the grant. The Exchequer equalisation grant was criticised on the following grounds:

(a) Even though a local authority did not receive a grant, the fact remained that it still lost three-quarters of its rates on industrial properties, and the whole of its rates on agricultural properties. The existing system took no account of this considerable loss of rateable value.

(b) Some authorities which were comparatively wealthy in rateable value had, as a result of not receiving a grant, to levy a higher rate than those which were in receipt of a grant. Here it must be noted that rateable value is not necessarily indicative of ability to pay, and thus individuals could be severely prejudiced by their authority not receiving a grant.

24. Report of the Working Party, 1953. The Working Party established to consider the operation of the Exchequer equalisation grant made the following observations, which were to form the basis of the rate deficiency grant of the *Local Government Act*, 1958:

(a) There was a need to limit the expenditure on which the grant was based in order to check extravagance.

(b) The "weighted population" concept should include a "sparsity" factor to deduct from density of population figures in the counties.

(c) There should be an interim grant, pending the operation of the new valuation list, to those authorities which received no grant at all, or one equal to less than a 1s. rate.

25. Local Government Act, 1958. The Act discontinued specific grants paid towards services such as education, local health services under the *National Health Service Act*, 1946, the fire service, child care (but not remand homes or approved schools) and town planning. The discontinued grants were replaced by a *general grant*. In addition the Act replaced the Exchequer equalisation grant with the *rate deficiency grant*.

26. The rate deficiency grant. This was distributed to all local authorities where the *product of a penny rate* per head of population was less than the average for the country.

Calculation was on a basis somewhat similar to that of the Exchequer equalisation grant, and operated as follows:

(a) The "weighted population" notion was only used in calculating the grant for the county councils, and a "sparsity of population" factor was incorporated.

(b) The *standard rate product* of the area was calculated by multiplying the average product of a penny rate per head for England and Wales by the population of the area, and, if this was less than the actual penny rate produced by the area, the difference was credited to the area.

(c) The expenditure of the area (less grants) was divided by the standard product of a penny rate to result in the number of penny rates necessary to be levied if the authority actually had a penny rate product per head equal to the national average.

(d) The grant then equalled the "credited" penny rate product multiplied by the number of penny rates as calculated in (c) above.

NOTE: Rate product was used under the 1958 Act as opposed to rateable value under the Act of 1948, and provisions were incorporated for limiting qualifying expenditure upon which the amount of the grant was based.

27. The general grant. In determining the amount available for the country as a whole the Minister must have regard to information available to him on the rate of relevant expenditure of local authorities and the level of prices, cost, remuneration and foreseeable future variations; any probable variation in demand for services giving rise to the relevant expenditure (where not under local authority control); the need to develop those services and the extent to which, having regard to economic conditions, it is convenient to do so.

Subject to approval by the House of Commons, the authorities' share of the aggregate amount was calculated on a formula:

(a) A *basic share* equal to a prescribed amount per head of weighted population was given.

(b) A *supplementary share* calculated by reference to such factors as children under five, density of population, school children, etc. was added.

(c) A *deduction* according to the value of a rate product was then made.

NOTE: The aggregate amount was fixed for two years but could be altered to take account of special changes.

THE PRESENT SYSTEM

28. The White Paper, 1966 (Cmnd. 2923). The Paper proposed among other things that a *rate support grant* should be introduced to replace the general and rate deficiency grants and some specific grants, and should be distributed to the major authorities on a basis of demographic and environmental factors, and to all authorities with below average rate resources.

It also commented on the lack of suitability of rates to carry the strain of local expenditure, but concluded that within the present structure of local government that there was no prospect of any major reform of local government finance.

29. The Rating Act, 1966. The Act attempts to reduce the burden of rates by making provisions for rebates in cases of low-income earners and for payment by instalments. It is essentially a measure to alleviate hardship until a more effective structure of local finance is evolved.

30. The Local Government Act, 1966. The Act introduced the rate support grant. The aggregate of the grant is divided into three elements:

(a) The *needs* element, which resembles the former general grant.

(b) The *resources* element, which resembles the old rate deficiency grant, with the exception that it is fixed in advance.

(c) The *domestic* element, which operates to relieve the burden of increasing rates by permitting reductions on dwelling-houses by 5d. in the £ for 1967–8, and 10d. for 1968–9, and on mixed hereditaments by 2d. and 5d. respectively.

31. Specific grants. These continue under the 1966 Act for housing and police, and new grants are made for the acquisition and development of land, for the payment of certain public health officials, and for special needs resulting from the existence of a large number of Commonwealth immigrants within a local authority.

NOTE: The 1966 Act is regarded merely as a temporary measure, until a new structure of local finance can be evolved in the light of changes recommended by the Royal Commission on local government in the structural aspects of local government.

RATES

32. General. Income from rates is a large part of local authority income, but a part which has been surpassed by grants since the mid-1930s. Its *basic importance* is that it provides local authorities with a source of income over which the central government has no direct control, and thus it forms the basis of local authority independence.

As will be seen, its *weakness* lies in its inflexibility and its regressive nature, and its growing failure to meet the ever-increasing demands of local expenditure. Its weaknesses have led the Minister of Housing and Local Government to say that "there is a need to overhaul local finance, including the abolition of rates, or there will be no future for local democracy."

33. Nature of rates. Rates are a tax levied by local authorities, with parliamentary consent, on the occupiers of real property inside the area of the local authority. They can be described as follows:

(*a*) They are a tax on the occupiers of real property, and not on the property itself.

(*b*) They are a tax on real property and not on personal property, except that plant and machinery are liable to rates.

NOTE: The value of the occupation for rating purposes depends on the annual letting value of the property concerned.

34. Amount of the local rate. This is determined by calculating the total proposed expenditure of the authority which is to be borne by the rates (*i.e.* excluding grants, trading receipts, etc.), and dividing this figure by the total rateable value of rateable properties (hereditaments) in the area. The resulting figure will be the *rate poundage* which is then borne by the individual occupiers according to their hereditaments individual rateable value.

35. Exemptions. The following classes of hereditaments are exempt from the payment of rates:

(*a*) *Crown property* occupied by servants of the Crown or by persons carrying out Crown functions though not technically Crown servants.

NOTE: In practice the Treasury will make a contribution in lieu of rates for *Crown property*, based on a valuation by the Treasury valuer (but these are completely *ex gratia*).

(*b*) *Charities* are eligible for rating relief of at least one-half of the rates they would otherwise be required to pay.

(*c*) *Agricultural land and buildings* are exempt, though agricultural dwelling-houses are not.

(*d*) *Places of public religious worship.*

(*e*) *Transport, electricity and gas* undertakings are technically exempt from the general rate structure, but pay rates based on special statutory formulae.

(*f*) *Voluntary and county schools.*

36. Machinery. Up to the *Local Government Act*, 1948, rating valuation was the responsibility of local authorities co-ordinated by *county valuation committees*. Since this date, however, valuation functions have been dealt with by the *Inland Revenue*.

(*a*) *Rating authorities.* The councils of county boroughs, boroughs, urban and rural districts are rating authorities.

(*b*) *Precepting authorities.* All other authorities are precepting authorities, *i.e.* they serve notice on the appropriate rating authority requiring it to levy a rate poundage in addition to its own rate to meet the requirements of the precepting authorities.

37. Determining annual value. Properties are either valued direct to their net annual value (or *rateable value*), or indirectly to gross annual value from which a statutory deduction is made to determine the net value:

(*a*) *Gross annual value.* This must be determined in the case of houses and non-industrial buildings and is defined as "the rent at which the hereditament might reasonably be expected to be let from year to year if the tenant undertook to pay all the usual tenant's rates and taxes and if the landlord bore the cost of repairs and insurance. . . ." (*Rating and Valuation Act*, 1925, *s.* 68).

(*b*) *Net annual value.* This is required for industrial buildings

E

and other buildings with land (other than gardens), and is the expected annual rent based on the same assumptions as in gross value, except that it is assumed that the cost of repairs and insurance is borne by the tenant (1925 Act, *s.* 22(1)(*b*)).

NOTE: in both cases a hypothetical tenancy and tenant are assumed for purposes of valuation.

APPRAISAL OF THE SYSTEM

38. General. The *Report of the Commissioners of Inland Revenue* for 1966 (Cmnd. 3200) revealed the following figures for the distribution of the burden of rates among different classes of rateable hereditaments:

Domestic properties   = 47·8 per cent
Commercial properties = 22·5 per cent
Industrial properties   = 14·8 per cent

The White Paper *Local Government Finance in England and Wales* (Cmnd. 2923) shows an *annual increase* in rates of between 9 per cent and 10 per cent, and comments that it appears that this trend is likely to increase or accelerate in the future: *e.g.* the average rate bill in 1956–7 amounted to £18 13*s.*, whereas the bill for 1966–7 amounted to £36 8*s.* It was also felt that averages were somewhat misleading as they do not emphasise that there is a large number of ratepayers paying well above the average, and that such persons are by no means always those who can best afford to do so.

39. Merits of the rating system.

(*a*) It is a comparatively *simple tax* to understand and has none of the financial and legal sophistications and intricacies of income tax.

(*b*) *National assessment* leads to a uniformity of standards existing in various areas.

(*c*) It is a *major independent* source of local revenue, conferring upon local authorities a certain measure of local discretion, within the limits of the law.

(*d*) It provides a *stable* source of income.

(*e*) It is reasonably *convenient* to administer and its cost of collection is correspondingly low.

(*f*) It requires large users of local services, *e.g.* large families, to bear part of the cost of such services, which is not necessarily the case with income tax.

(*g*) It leads to the better and more *economic use of property* by encouraging persons not to occupy property larger than they really need.

(*h*) It involves a *lack of intrusion* into private affairs, unlike income tax.

40. Disadvantages of the rating system. These suggested merits of the rating system, some of which are in any case rather specious, pale into insignificance beside its obvious disadvantages set out in **41** and **42** below.

41. Rates not related to income.

(*a*) *Regressive nature.* Rates are not based on ability to pay and it is inaccurate to try to correlate wealth with the size of a person's living accommodation. Unlike income tax which graduates upwards according to increases in income (*i.e. a progressive tax*) rates bear no relation to a person's income.

NOTE: The *Allen Committee* pointed out that rates as a percentage of household income amounted to between 6 and 18 per cent in the lower income groups, but only to about 1·8 to 3 per cent in incomes of over £1,560 p.a.

(*b*) *Inequitable.* Although disparities have been reduced by the rebate scheme of the *Rating Act*, 1966, a gulf still exists, particularly between the upper reaches of the low income groups who do not qualify for rebates, and those with higher incomes.

(*c*) Rate income fails to keep pace with increases in personal income.

42. Other disadvantages.

(*a*) *Increased costs.* The continually increasing costs of the services is borne to a large extent by the householder; and, despite the fact that only a small proportion of total rate income is paid by the poorer ratepayers, it causes them considerable hardship.

(*b*) *Industrial and commercial properties.* These can obtain relief on their rate payments through the tax system, and through the possibility of passing on rates to the consumer in higher prices.

(*c*) *Disparities.* There is a wide disparity in rateable resources between areas, which means increasing government aid to the less well endowed authorities.

(*d*) *Rural areas.* The de-rating of agricultural land is a historical anomaly and deprives rural areas of a considerable rate income.

(*e*) *Inflexibility.* Rates are not easily adjusted to changing conditions.

(*f*) *Miscellaneous.* In addition to the above disadvantages, rates are often criticised on the grounds that they deter the improving of property, and bear no relation to the amount of use made of local services.

BORROWING

43. Internal funds. Local authorities have the power (*Local Authorities Loans Act*, 1948) to invest surpluses on "capital funds" internally for statutory borrowing purposes. Specific powers exist also under the *Local Government Superannuation Act*, 1937, and the *Housing (Financial Provisions) Act*, 1958.

Such capital funds include superannuation funds, repair and renewal of property funds, and special funds instituted for future expenditure. These lending funds have a right to immediate repayment should the need arise, and must be paid the rate of interest paid on council mortgages.

Many authorities use the method of providing in the rates for part of their future capital expenditure, and this "pay as you go" policy has been approved by the Minister, though subject to limits on the rate poundage used for it.

44. When is borrowing necessary? Where the benefit of local authority capital expenditure is to be felt over a number of years, and where the charging of an item to any one year would place a considerable burden on the rates, borrowing is necessary, for instance:

(*a*) Acquiring of realisable assets, *e.g.* houses.
(*b*) Expenditure on trading undertakings.
(*c*) Assets for community benefit, *e.g.* sewers.
(*d*) Capital expenditure which provides no lasting tangible benefit, *e.g.* promotion of a private bill.

45. External borrowing. The use of internal funds mentioned above only provides a small proportion of the necessary borrowing, *i.e.* 6·2 per cent in 1960, and only 4·7 per cent in 1965. Use must therefore be made of outside sources. The principal external sources are:

(*a*) *Public Works Loan Board.* This is a rapidly diminishing source of revenue, having decreased from 65·5 per cent in 1955 to 33·3 per cent in 1965. It is an independent statutory body appointed by the Crown "to consider loan applications from local authorities." It is financed by government loans and its rate of interest is fixed by the Treasury. It is very much subject to government financial policy, *e.g.* between 1945 and 1952 only the smaller authorities without the power to borrow in the open market could use it.

From 1952 to 1960 it has acted as the "lender of the last resort" with rates of interest equated to market rates, thus forcing authorities into the short-term money market and leading to the creation of a secondary London money market to finance this demand.

Since 1964 an increased amount has been advanced, but only up to a certain proportion of an authority's total borrowing.

(*b*) *Mortgages.* This source has increased from 14 per cent in 1955 to 28·4 per cent at present. They are subscribed mainly by the mortgage market and individual investors, and give a yield of 7 to 7½ per cent according to duration, etc. They are made on the security of the local rates.

(*c*) *Temporary money.* This consists of loans and overdrafts for a period of under one year, and represents 22 per cent of local borrowing. There is also an increasing excursion into the "overnight" market, owing to the considerable interest savings which may be made. This is however limited by the lack of staff to deal with it.

(*d*) *Stock.* This has remained constant at around 9 to 10 per cent, but its attraction of appealing to a wide market is offset by the high rates of interest involved.

INCOME FROM TRADING, ETC.

46. Trading services. Municipal trading developed largely from the provision of services which local authorities undertook as a result of new social conditions: *e.g.* provision of water, electricity and gas.

Socialist ideals involving the municipalisation of various services and provision of consumer goods have not been widely adopted. The principal local authority trading activities are generally nowadays confined to municipal transport services, and such lesser items as swimming pools and recreational facilities, for which charges are made.

47. The problem of trading services. At present local trading services provide a very small proportion of local revenue, and an increase in the future seems highly improbable. The main problem seems to be that of determining on what basis such services should be run: should they be run for profit and used to keep down the rates, or should they be run to provide amenities with charges limited to a nominal amount, or merely enough to cover running expenses?

In addition they are limited to the area of the local authority and have to face competition from large-scale industrial firms. This also raises the problem of whether they should be supplementary to private enterprise, or run in direct competition with it.

48. Non-trading services. Income from miscellaneous sources amounting to approximately 30 per cent of local authority income comes principally from the rents of council houses. However, such rents are not "economic" in the normal sense of the term, and as such do not represent a *real* increase in local authority income; in fact they are the result of increased expenditure by the authority in providing the housing.

CONCLUSIONS

49. Conclusion on grants. It is an accepted general position in unitary as opposed to federal states that control of taxation must lie with the central government, and that local authorities may only have delegated taxing powers which are of necessity limited in scope.

NOTE: In the USA, owing to the wider local taxing powers, central grants have declined as a proportion of local revenue from 70 per cent in 1915 to 33 per cent in 1960.

50. The Maud Committee. The committee has recommended the establishment of management boards which will be responsible, *inter alia*, for the integration of local financial decisions, and will stress the financial implications of the capital and current expenditure of the authority.

51. Alternative taxes in the USA. The following local taxes are levied in various parts of the USA: local income tax in Philadelphia, St. Louis and Washington D.C.; retail sales taxes of 2 per cent in Kansas; and variations of personal and corporation income taxes, death and gift taxes, general sales, alcohol, tobacco, motor fuel, motor vehicles and payroll taxes.

52. Alternative sources of revenue. The following have been suggested but not yet adopted in England and Wales:

(a) *Charge for local services.* Charges on a basis of user have been suggested, but would suffer from considerable social and political objections.

(b) *Site value rating.* This is proposed by the Liberal Party, and it is claimed would give a higher yield and reduce the domestic burden. Properties would be rated on a site value basis and not on a rental basis, thus making shops and offices near town centres bear a higher part of the cost.

(c) *Ending of de-rating.* It is claimed this would add £100 million—but that is only enough to meet one normal annual increase in the total rate bill.

(d) *Local income tax.* This raises problems as to basis of such a tax, whether on residence or place of work, and in duplicating the national system could have considerable disincentive effects.

(e) *Trading.* Increase in municipal trading.

(f) *Local sales taxes.* These are not really feasible, as control of taxation levels is a potent economic regulator and must remain in the hands of the central government.

NOTE: Other possibilities include the transfer of services to the state, in particular education, which is largely state-supported in any case.

LOCAL AUDIT

53. District audit. Under the *Local Government Act*, 1933, the system of district audit, *i.e.* audit of local authority accounts by professionally qualified auditors of the Ministry of Housing and Local Government, is applied to the accounts of county councils, the GLC, the London borough councils, district councils, parish councils and meetings, to the accounts of joint authorities and to certain accounts which are made subject to district audit by statutory order.

Boroughs and county boroughs are excluded from the system, unless they specifically resolve to adopt it, but such accounts as rate collection, education and children's service accounts are subject to it.

(a) *Nature of the audit.* The district auditor will examine accounts both from the strictly accounting aspect, and also from the legal aspect to determine the legality of all payments made by the authority.

(b) *Powers of auditor.* In addition to the power to compel the production of all relevant documents, the auditor may disallow all payments made without legal authority, and surcharge the individual members responsible for agreeing to such payments. The effect of *disallowance and surcharge* is to render the individual member liable to make up the deficit, unless the payment is *sanctioned* by the Minister, or unless a successful appeal is brought in the High Court (for over £500) or to the Minister or High Court (for under £500).

54. Borough audit. Boroughs and county boroughs are exempt from the system of district audit, unless they specifically adopt it, this led to the comment by Farwell, J. in *A.-G.* v. *De Winton* (1906) that "it is difficult to understand why the legislature . . . should have authorised a system of auditing which is quite illusory . . . when they had seven years before created an efficient method."

What is this *"illusory" method* ? A borough has a choice between the following types of audit:

(a) *Elective audit.* Three auditors are appointed, two being elected by the local electors, and one chosen by the mayor from among council members. They have no power of surcharge; need not be professionally qualified or even competent; and have no binding duty to disclose errors.

(b) *Professional audit.* Auditors may be appointed belonging to recognised professional bodies, and although having the power to compel production of books, etc., and the duty to make such observations in their report as they think fit, there is no power of disallowance and surcharge.

PROGRESS TEST 9

1. What are the general principles of local government finance? **(1, 2)**

2. What is the basic financial problem?   **(3)**

3. Outline the financial procedure of local authorities.   **(4–8)**

4. Why are central government grants-in-aid of local authorities made?   **(9, 10)**

5. What arguments may be made in principle against the grant system?   **(11)**

6. What general principles should underlie a system of central government grants?   **(12)**

7. What are the main types of grant?   **(13, 14)**

8. Outline the development of the grant system down to 1948. **(15–19)**

9. What were the grant provisions of the *Local Government Act,* 1948? (**21, 22**)

10. What alterations were made to the grant system by the *Local Government Act,* 1958? (**25, 26**)

11. Describe the present system of grants. (**28–30**)

12. Outline the nature of local rates. (**33**)

13. How is the amount of the rate fixed? (**34–37**) What exemptions and reliefs exist? (**35**)

14. What merits has the rating system? (**39**)

15. What are the disadvantages of the rating system? (**40–42**)

16. What role do internal funds play as a source of local authority borrowing? (**43**)

17. Why do local authorities borrow? (**44**)

18. Describe the principal sources of external borrowing. (**45**)

19. What is the role of municipal trading as a source of revenue, and what problems attend it? (**46–48**)

20. What alternatives exist to the present system of finance? (**51, 52**)

21. Describe the system of district audit. (**53**)

22. What types of audit are available to a borough? (**54**)

CHAPTER X

THE FUNCTIONS OF LOCAL AUTHORITIES

ACQUISITION OF POWERS

1. The source of local authority functions. All local authority powers must stem from some statutory authorisation, otherwise the actions of a local authority will be *ultra vires* and illegal. Most local powers stem from the provisions of some general statute, *e.g.* the *Public Health Act*, 1936, or from private legislation. In addition powers may be available under the general law subject to the taking of some special procedure, or under the system of the preparation of schemes (*see* VII, **25**). The various methods are described in **2** below.

2. Forms of authorisation.

(*a*) *Private legislation.* All local authorities, except parish councils, have a power to promote private Bills in order to confer upon themselves powers in addition to those granted by the general law.

(*b*) *Adoptive Acts.* A popular method in the earlier history of local government, but one which is losing favour at the present day, is that of making a statute effective within an area only when it is formally adopted by the local authority. An example is the use of the Private Street Works Codes now contained in the *Highways Act*, 1959.

(*c*) *Orders subject to special parliamentary procedure.* During the nineteenth century the method of the *provisional order* was introduced to enable local authorities to gain powers without the expense of a private Act. Application was made to the appropriate department, and after an inquiry, the request could be incorporated in a provisional order, which could be petitioned against before being confirmed by Act of Parliament. This procedure has been effectively replaced under the *Statutory Orders (Special Procedure) Act*, 1945, which enables a ministerial order to become operative at the end of a fixed objection period.

(*d*) *Ministerial order.* In certain cases a statutory provision only becomes operative in the area of a local authority after an appropriate ministerial order has been made: *e.g.* the conferring of certain powers upon rural authorities, particularly certain public health functions under the *Public Health Acts* of 1875 and 1936.

(*e*) *Statutory schemes.* These are dealt with in VII, **25.**

EDUCATION

3. The basis of the function. In England and Wales expenditure on education is by far the greatest single outlay by local authorities, amounting in 1964–5 to £1,485 million. In 1965 there were seven million pupils in maintained primary and secondary schools.

However, education was on a voluntary basis until the middle of the nineteenth century, and the first government grants—made in 1833 to the *National Society* and to the *British and Foreign Schools Society*—amounted to a mere £20,000. The *Education Act*, 1870, set up *School Boards* in areas without adequate schools and authorised the raising of a rate. It also established *compulsory education* for the 5–13 age group. The *Education Act*, 1902, made *counties* and *county boroughs* education authorities, and boroughs with over 10,000, and districts with over 20,000 responsible for elementary education only.

4. Subsequent developments. The *Education Act*, 1918, strengthened local authorities, raised grant assistance to 50 per cent, abolished fees, extended the range of permissive services, and raised the leaving age to 14. The Act made counties and county boroughs responsible for "establishing a national system of education."

5. The Education Act, 1944. This Act set up the modern system. Section 1 established the Ministry of Education (now the *Department of Education and Science*) as the central administrative body with the duty of "promoting the education of the people of England and Wales and the progressive development of institutions devoted to that purpose . . . and to secure the execution of national policy for providing a varied and comprehensive education service through the authorities under his control." The Minister was given extensive powers of direction (*s.* 68), of appellate jurisdiction (*s.* 67), and inspection (*s.* 77).

6. Local administration. The councils of *counties* and *county boroughs* are local education authorities, subject to the power of the Secretary of State to create joint boards where he considers it desirable. The counties may partition their areas into divisions for efficient and convenient administration, and may constitute *divisional executives* to whom functions may be delegated.

7. Excepted districts. Urban and rural districts whose populations in 1939 exceeded 30,000, or who had 7,000 pupils on the rolls of public elementary schools, were placed outside the general structure and constituted as local education authorities. Under the *Local Government Act*, 1958, a new claim for "excepted" status may be made by boroughs and urban districts with a population of over 60,000.

8. Committees. Each local education authority must appoint an education committee containing co-opted persons of specialised knowledge to work in co-operation with the *chief education officer*.

9. Classification. Local authority schools are classified into the following groups:

(*a*) *Primary.* Up to the age of 11.

(*b*) *Secondary.* Between the ages of 11 and 15, and including secondary technical and secondary modern education.

NOTE: Following the Ministry circular 10/65, local authorities are under a duty to prepare schemes for ending selection and for eliminating the separation in secondary education. Local authorities must submit plans for the reorganisation of secondary education in their area on comprehensive lines.

(*c*) *Further stage.* This includes county colleges, colleges of art and of commerce, evening institutes, adult education and youth services.

10. Duties. Local education authorities are under a duty to ensure that sufficient schools exist in their areas, with regard being paid to the need for nursery schools, special schools, and boarding accommodation.

The *administration* of primary and secondary schools is shared between the authority and the *managers* (primary schools) or *governors* (secondary schools). Secular education is under the control of the authority, except in *aided* secondary schools. Religious education must conform to the approval of a conference convened by the local education authority with representatives of local religious bodies.

11. Appointment of teachers. The authority controls the appointment and dismissal of teachers in county schools, special agreement and controlled schools; though in the last two cases the governing body must be satisfied as to the competence of the persons appointed.

12. Further education. Every local education authority is under a duty to secure the provision of satisfactory facilities for further education. This means full- and part-time education for persons over school leaving age, and leisure-time occupation in organised centres for those over school leaving, and able and willing to profit by it.

13. Ancillary functions. In addition to the provision of schools and the appointment of teachers, etc. the local education authority has important responsibilities for ancillary duties concerned with education, the more important being:

(a) The youth employment service.
(b) Medical inspection.
(c) Clothing, milk and meals.
(d) Recreation and social and physical training.
(e) Employment of children and young persons.
(f) Provision of transport facilities.
(g) Teacher training.

HOUSING

14. Housing authorities. The councils of boroughs, urban and rural districts are housing authorities. In the City of London the Common Council is the authority, and in Greater London the principal housing authorities are the London boroughs, with limited functions, *e.g.* overspill housing, reserved to the Greater London Council. The Minister principally responsible is the Minister of Housing and Local Government assisted by a Central Housing Advisory Committee.

15. Provision of accommodation. A housing authority is under a duty to carry out periodical reviews of the housing needs of its area, and may provide accommodation by the following methods:

    (a) By acquiring houses.
    (b) By erecting houses on local authority land.
    (c) By conversions, alterations, enlarging, repairing, or improving buildings acquired by the authority.

In support of these powers the authority is empowered to provide shops, recreation grounds and other environmental amenities.

NOTE: In rural areas the county council is required to make a constant review of the housing conditions.

16. Management. The housing authority has "management and control" of its houses.

    (a) It may do "such acts as may fairly be regarded as acts of management by a landlord in the ordinary sense of the term" (*A.-G.* v. *Crayford UDC* (1962)).

    (b) *Rents* are within the discretion of the authority, provided that they are "reasonable" and are regularly reviewed.

    (c) In *selecting tenants* the authority must act in accordance with the Housing Acts giving priorities to particular classifications.

17. Functions under the Housing Act, 1957. These cover individual premises or groups of premises, and are described in **18** and **19** below.

18. Individual premises.

    (a) *Dilapidated houses.* Where a house may be deemed "*unfit*" within the statutory definition of the term (*Housing Act*, 1957, *s.* 4) the authority is accorded certain powers either to deal with the premises as a *single unit* or as part of a *group of premises.* In the former case its powers are further divided according to whether or not the property can be repaired at reasonable cost.

    (b) *Individual premises repairable at reasonable cost.* These may be dealt with in the following ways:

        (i) By issue of a *repair notice* (*s.* 9).
        (ii) By execution of the work in default of a repair notice, and by recovering the cost from the owner (*s.* 10).

(c) *Premises not repairable at reasonable cost.* The authority may:

(i) Accept an undertaking from the owner to repair, or

(ii) Make a *demolition order* requiring the demolishing of the building and clearing of the site, or

(iii) Make a *closing order* forbidding the house or part thereof to be used for human habitation.

19. Groups of premises. These may be dealt with in the following ways, generally classified as *"slum clearance."*

(a) *Clearance area.* Where houses in an area are unfit for human habitation, or are a danger to health because of the bad arrangement of the area, and the only solution is that of complete demolition, the authority may resolve that the area be declared a clearance area, provided:

(i) That its resources are sufficient, and

(ii) That suitable alternative accommodation is available. If the action is confirmed by the Minister, the authority may proceed by *clearance order* which obliges owners to clear the sites, or by *compulsory purchase order* (the choice being clearly at the authority's discretion).

NOTE: The clearance area procedure will generally be used where the environmental conditions are so bad that it is imperative that the inhabitants should be housed away from the area. Where, however, it is socially desirable to keep the inhabitants near their place of work, etc., the following procedure could be used.

(b) *Re-development areas.* This enables the authority to take steps in areas of overcrowded, unfit or congested working-class houses. The authority, by resolving the area to be a re-development area, and by obtaining ministerial confirmation, will acquire the land by agreement or compulsory purchase. It will then redevelop the site. Note that this procedure has been effectively replaced by the comprehensive development area provisions of the *Town and Country Planning Act*, 1962.

(c) *Overcrowding.* The housing authority is under a duty to review its area for the existence of overcrowding, and to submit proposals to the Minister for its abatement. They may, however, temporarily licence overcrowding in certain cases.

20. The Housing Act, 1964. The principal feature of the 1964 Act was the introduction of a procedure for compulsory improvement of dwellings (though repeal and replacement by stronger provisions is now urged). The system of voluntary improvement grants in operation (*see* below) had proved ineffective to bring the 2½ million "twilight" dwellings in England and Wales up to an approved standard. In particular voluntary grants had proved ineffective in the case of landlord-controlled property. The Act aimed at improving the so-called twilight dwellings up to a standard where they could provide satisfactory living accommodation for at least fifteen years.

21. Compulsory improvement areas. The Act enables local authorities to declare an area a compulsory improvement area, and to secure the improvement of dwellings within the area. Improvement notices may be served, which may be suspended for up to five years (but not in the case of tenement blocks), compelling the owner to improve the house up to the full or reduced standard of amenities (*see* below). Note that the tenant may also request the authority to compel the landlord to carry out necessary improvements.

22. Improvement grants. The *Housing (Financial Provisions) Act*, 1958, and the *Housing Act*, 1959, introduced a system of discretionary grants in the former case, and obligatory grants in the latter.

The 1958 Act authorised the making of grants towards the cost of converting existing houses, so as to provide additional accommodation, whereas the 1959 Act obliged local authorities to make *standard grants* towards the cost of installing certain standard amenities: *e.g.* a fixed bath or shower, a water closet and a piped water supply. In order to qualify for a grant, the dwelling had to be equipped with all the standard amenities when the work was completed. However, the *Housing Act*, 1964, now provides that the standard grant may be for a *reduced standard of amenities*.

23. Houses in multiple occupation. Under the *Housing Act*, 1961, powers of management were conferred upon local authorities for houses in multiple occupation and tenement blocks. The Minister prescribed a *code of management* which the authority can apply to such premises, and which covers such matters as drainage, water supply, common facilities and refuse disposal. The authority may require the execution of works in such premises (apart from the code), and the provision of fire escapes, limitations on the number of inhabitants, and a scheme for the registration of such premises. The *Housing Act*, 1964, extends the power of the local authorities by enabling them to make a *control order* in cases of emergency, which has the effect of putting the authority in immediate control of the property, and enabling them to take on the role of the dispossessed owner and carry out the works required by the management order.

24. Other functions.

(*a*) *House purchase.* Local authorities are empowered to make loans on mortgage for the purpose of house purchase, a facility which is much reduced in times of national stringency.

(*b*) *Housing associations.* Local authorities are empowered to assist local housing associations to provide housing accommodation through loans, advice and the acquisition of land. At a central level such associations are assisted by the *Housing Corporation* set up under the *Housing Act,* 1964.

(*c*) *Rent Act*, 1965. Local authorities are given important administrative functions as to the regulation of tenancies and the registration of rents of controlled dwellings.

TOWN AND COUNTRY PLANNING

25. Background. A feature of towns developed as the result of the industrial revolution was the general absence of planned layout and construction. The *Town Planning Act*, 1909, enabled local authorities to prepare schemes for undeveloped areas, but was generally concerned (as was subsequent legislation) with the control of land use rather than with positive aspects of planning. The *Barlow Report* (1940) on the Location of Industry and the Distribution of the Industrial Population, and the *Scott Report* (1942) on Land Utilisation in Rural Areas, followed by the *Uthwatt Report* (1941) led to the creation of a Minister of Town and Country Planning in 1943, and the Act of 1944 enabling local authorities to purchase land for planning purposes.

26. Planning authorities. The *Town and Country Planning Act*, 1947, constituted county and county borough councils as local planning authorities, subject to powers of delegation, and to the right of county districts with populations exceeding 60,000 to claim delegated powers.

27. The development plan. The basis of planning control and development in any area is the development plan. The plan will define proposed future uses of land in the area of the authority, and must divide the area into residential, agricultural and industrial uses.

It will also designate as subject to compulsory purchase land in an *area of comprehensive development, i.e.* an area which the planning authority considers should be developed as a whole to deal satisfactorily with such matters as war damage, obsolete development, or bad layout, or to provide for the relocation of population or industry, or for the replacement of open spaces, or for other specified purposes.

NOTE: The county council in preparing the plan does not have unfettered discretion as it must:

(*i*) Consult the district councils in its area.
(*ii*) Make the plan according to general ministerial directions as to matters which may be included or which must be included.
(*iii*) The completed plan is subject to ministerial approval.
(*iv*) Prepare a fresh survey every five years.

28. Control of development. Under Part III of the 1962 *Town and Country Planning Act*, and the regulations made under it, control of development is effected by local planning authorities. Here the duties of the local authority are as follows:

(*a*) To determine whether a proposed development constitutes *development* within the meaning of the Act.
(*b*) To consent or withhold consent according to the merits and desirability of the proposed development.

PUBLIC HEALTH

29. Public health authorities. The councils of county boroughs, boroughs, urban and rural districts are public health authorities. In London the authorities are the Common Council of the City of London and the London borough councils, subject to the reservation of certain functions to the Greater

London Council, *e.g.* refuse disposal and the provision of main sewers and sewage disposal works.

In addition the Minister may constitute a union of districts as a joint public health authority, provided the initiative stems from one or more of the districts concerned. Also certain public health functions may be discharged by port health authorities.

30. Public health functions. The principal functions of local public health authorities are set out in **31–33** below.

31. Effluent disposal.

(*a*) *Sewers and drains.* The former are defined in the *Public Health Act*, 1936, as pipes used for the drainage of buildings not within the same curtilage; the latter as pipes used for the drainage of a single building or buildings within the same curtilage. *Drains* are basically a *private* responsibility subject to the rights of the local authority to ensure adequate drainage under the Act of 1936, and its right to deal with stopped-up drains under the *Public Health Act*, 1961. *Sewers* may be a *public or private* responsibility according to whether they were built before 1937 or have been subsequently adopted. Where they are a public responsibility, the authority is under a duty to ensure that it provides public sewers adequate for the effective draining of its area, and must maintain, empty and clean, such sewers.

(*b*) *Trade effluents.* The authority may make regulations on the discharge of trade effluents into public sewers, and may make appropriate charges.

(*c*) *Sewage disposal.* Every authority is under a duty to deal effectively with the contents of its sewers by means of sewage disposal works.

32. Buildings and sites. Local public health authorities have considerable powers to ensure the adequacy and sanitary condition of buildings and sites within its area, and these can be exercised in the following ways:

(*a*) *Building regulations.* Any person undertaking works on a building must submit appropriate plans to the local authority. Where the plans conform to the building regulations, laid down by the Minister under the *Public Health Act*, 1961, the authority has no alternative but to approve them. In other cases the authority must reject plans: *e.g.* where the building is over a sewer, or where there is insufficient access for refuse removal, or where the means of ingress and egress to a public building are inadequate. In other cases the authorities are given dispensing powers.

(b) *Safety and amenity*. The authority may require the removal of, or the carrying out of works at, dangerous premises, and are entitled to take immediate action in cases of danger. In addition the authority exercises control over demolition works, and when granting permission for demolition may make conditions as to the shoring up of adjacent buildings, removal of rubbish, etc.

The authority may also deal with ruinous buildings which are detrimental to the amenities of the neighbourhood. It may apply for a closing order for a building used for public entertainment without sufficient means of access, and it is responsible for requiring the provision of fire escapes in certain buildings where required by statute.

33. Nuisances and other functions.

(a) *Statutory nuisances*. It is the duty of the local authority to inspect its area for the detection of statutory nuisances as defined in the *Public Health Act*, 1936 (*s.* 92), which include premises in such a state as to be prejudicial to health or a nuisance; accumulations or deposits prejudicial to health, etc. In addition under the *Clean Air Act*, 1956, the emission of smoke in certain circumstances may be a nuisance, and under the *Noise Abatement Act*, 1960, noise or vibration can constitute a statutory nuisance. Proceedings may be instituted through magistrates' courts under the 1936 Act, or under the expedited procedure of the 1961 Act in cases of emergency.

(b) *Offensive trades*. The authority is responsible for the granting of permission for the carrying on of such trades and for the making of bye-laws for them.

(c) *Refuse collection*. A local authority may undertake, or may be required by the Minister to undertake, the removal of house refuse, or the removal (with a charge) of trade refuse.

(d) *Miscellaneous powers*. The authority is also responsible for such matters as:

　(i) Rat control.
　(ii) Inspection of nursing homes.
　(iii) Mortuaries.
　(iv) Caravan site regulation.

HIGHWAYS

34. Authorities. Division of responsibilities for highways depends upon the nature of the particular highways in the area of each authority. *County boroughs* are responsible for all high-ways in their area, with the exception of trunk roads which are the responsibility of the *Ministry of Transport*. *County councils* are responsible for all roads in rural districts and for *classified* roads in other districts. However, under the *Highways Act*, 1959, boroughs and urban districts with a population of over 20,000 may claim the right to maintain classified roads in their areas, otherwise they will be responsible for all *unclassified* roads in their areas. A county council may *delegate* powers over roads which cannot be *claimed*, and in rural districts.

In *Greater London* the GLC is the highway authority for *metropolitan* roads, and the London boroughs, etc. are respon-sible for all others which are not the responsibility of the Ministry.

35. Duties of highway authorities. Highways which were created under the *Highways Act*, 1835, or created subsequently, are the responsibility of the highway authority and repairable at public expense. Similarly, public paths, etc. created under the *National Parks and Access to the Countryside Act*, 1949, are so repairable. The duty of the authority is to maintain its roads in a state suitable to meet the needs of the traffic which is reasonably likely to use them.

Responsibility for *bridges* lies with the authority responsible for the highway which crosses the bridge.

36. Enforcement of the duty. A person may serve notice on the local authority requiring repairs to a highway, and in default may seek an order of enforcement from Quarter Sessions. If the extent of the liability is disputed, the matter may be settled by a magistrates' court, or where liability is denied a High Court declaration may be sought.

37. Particular aspects. There are various other matters over which a highway authority has responsibilities. They are as follows:

(a) *Private streets.* For streets where there is no one who can specifically be compelled to undertake ordinary repairs, the highway authority may carry out repairs in emergency and charge the frontagers, or may take steps for permanent making-up and adoption under the Private Street Works Codes contained in the *Highways Act*, 1959, as supplemented by the Advance Payments Code.

(b) *Diversion and extinguishment.* Highway authorities may take steps in a magistrates' court for the diversion or extinguishment of roads under its control.

(c) *Lighting.* It is responsible for the *lighting and cleansing* of its roads.

(d) *Nuisances.* It must take steps to abate nuisances affecting highways.

HEALTH AND WELFARE SERVICES

38. System under the National Health Service Act, 1946. The Act evolved a tripartite scheme involving the following services:

(a) *Hospitals and specialist services.* These are the responsibility of the Minister acting through hospital management committees under the control of regional hospital boards.

(b) *Personal health services.* These are provided in the patients' homes, and are administered by local authorities: *county councils, county boroughs, London boroughs* and *the Common Council of the City.*

(c) *General services.* General medical, dental, pharmaceutical and ophthalmic services are administered by various special bodies, *e.g.* executive councils.

39. Duties of the authorities. Under Part III of the Act the following duties are imposed upon local authorities:

(a) *Health centres.* Authorities must provide centres, and equipment and maintenance of centres, at which facilities for general medical, dental and other facilities may be provided. The staffing and providing of services is not the responsibility of the authorities.

NOTE: The provision of centres has been slow, and the *Guillebaud Committee* (1956) has suggested that equal benefits could be obtained by more efficient use of existing local centres.

(b) *Maternity and child welfare.* This includes the securing of adequate midwives and the care of expectant mothers.

(c) *Home nursing.*

(d) *Employment of health visitors.* To give advice to children, expectant and nursing mothers, etc.

(e) *Ambulance services.* The authority must provide an adequate ambulance service for the area.

In addition the following permissive powers exist:

(*f*) *Mental health.* To give care and after-care, involving residential accommodation, training facilities and the appointment of welfare officers (largely governed by the *Mental Health Act,* 1959).

(*g*) *Domestic help.* This may be provided where appropriate.

(*h*) Services for the elderly and for the handicapped.

40. Services under the National Assistance Act, 1948. The principal functions under the Act include the following:

(*a*) *The provision of accommodation.* Residential accommodation must be provided for the aged, the infirm, and the mentally ill; and temporary accommodation for those suffering from misfortune.

(*b*) *Provision of welfare services.* Arrangements must be made for promoting the welfare of persons suffering from handicaps, such as the blind, the deaf or the dumb, or for mentally disordered persons. This may include recreational facilities, workshops and hostels.

41. Child care. The councils of counties, county boroughs and the London boroughs are responsible for administering the statutory provisions concerned with child welfare; the principal ones are the *Children Act,* 1948, the *Adoption Act,* 1950, the *Children and Young Persons Acts,* 1933–1963, the *Children Act,* 1958, and the *Mental Health Act,* 1959.

The main duties imposed on the local authorities are given in **42** below.

42. Principal duties of local authorities.

(*a*) *Adoption.* Local authorities may act as adoption societies, must register adoption societies on approval, and may be called upon to represent children in adoption proceedings.

(*b*) *Child protection.* Local authorities have a duty to see to the well-being of foster children, to secure the well-being of "*protected*" children, to keep a register of, and approve of, nurseries, and to inspect premises used for housing foster children, refusing permission if circumstances are unsuitable.

(*c*) *Deprived children.* The authorities are required to care for children under the age of 17 who are without parents or guardians, or where the parents or guardians are incapable of caring for the children, provided that to do so is in the best interests of the child.

(d) *Remand homes and approved schools.* Health authorities must provide remand homes for children sent to them as a punishment, and may be required to provide approved schools for children who have committed an offence for which an adult may be imprisoned.

(e) *Mental health.* Duties include the care and visiting of children suffering from mental disorders.

(f) *Care or protection, or control.* Powers are conferred on local authorities to deal with children in need of care, protection, or control: *e.g.* children having bad associates, or being part of a household where another member has been convicted of an offence against a child.

POLICE AND FIRE SERVICES

43. Police authorities. The councils of counties and county boroughs, or an amalgamated area, form police areas, with the appropriate authority being the *watch committee* in the borough, the *police committee* in the county, or the authority set up by an amalgamation scheme.

44. Duty of the authority. The management of the police force is generally controlled by the regulations of the Home Secretary. Under the *Police Act*, 1964, the duties of the authority are limited to maintaining the force and providing adequate equipment, the appointment of a chief constable and the establishment of a police fund. General operative management is in the hands of the chief constable.

45. Fire service authorities. The councils of counties, county boroughs and the Greater London Council are fire service authorities, subject to considerable powers of regulation by the Secretary of State.

MISCELLANEOUS SERVICES

46. General. The following services are dealt with in brief. However, this should not be taken to mean that they lack importance.

(a) *Recreational services.* These include the provision of libraries, museums, parks and recreation grounds, allotments, public entertainment and swimming baths.

(b) *Civil Defence.* (To be ended as an economy measure.)

(c) *Food and drugs.* Duties relating to offences, registration of dairies, control of markets.

(d) *Shops.* Closing hours, Sunday trading and conditions of employment are within the responsibility of the local authority.

(e) *Testing of weights and measures.*

(f) Water resources, river pollution, land drainage and coast protection.

(g) Local land charges registration.

47. Conclusions. The following points may usefully be noted from a study of functions:

(a) The extremely wide range of local authority functions, covering a great number of aspects of everyday life.

(b) The tendency to concentrate the most important powers in the hands of the larger authorities.

(c) The lack of any methodical distribution of functions based on population, areas, or resources.

PROGRESS TEST 10

1. How do local authorities acquire their powers? **(1, 2)**

2. Outline the education service of local authorities. **(3, 4, 8, 9–13)**

3. What is the local authority educational structure? **(4–7)**

4. What are the principal functions of local housing authorities in connection with the provision of accommodation? **(14–16)**

5. What are the principal functions under the *Housing Acts*, 1957 and 1964? **(17–23)**

6. Which authorities exercise planning functions, and what are their principal functions? **(26–28)**

7. What are the principal public health responsibilities of a local authority? **(29–33)**

8. Which authorities are highway authorities, and what are their major functions? **(34, 35)**

9. Outline the health and welfare services provided by a local authority. **(38–42)**

10. Outline the police and fire services. **(44, 45)**

11. What conclusions may be drawn from a study of local functions? **(47)**

LOCAL GOVERNMENT ELECTIONS

PARTY POLITICS IN LOCAL GOVERNMENT

1. General. Party political organisations are not found throughout local government, and local party divisions are not always the same as those obtaining in national politics: *e.g.* in London until 1946 the Conservatives were not described as such, and there are a large number of Conservative fringe groups passing under different names.

Scope for independents still exists; in 1966 three county councils had independent majorities, and one was wholly composed of independents. In addition 20 per cent of non-county boroughs were organized on non-party lines. However the practice of political division is growing, and this is fostered and encouraged by the national press devoting considerable attention and significance to local results as indicative of national trends, even though the extent of this is often slight. Here the elections in London have been of particular significance.

2. Influence of party politics. Whatever view one holds on whether party politics should be an important or a proper force in local government, it must be recognised that its influence is growing. Except in certain rural areas, local elections are now generally fought on party lines, and the crux of the matter is not whether local political divisions exist, but the amount of influence which they have for good or ill on local administration, particularly through the disciplining and regimentation of members.

3. General advantage of local political parties.

(*a*) *Nature of issues.* A large number of the crucial issues in local government at the present day are closely related to national policy on the same issues. Particularly is this so in such matters as housing and education. Local government thus being concerned with the local appl:cation of national policies, local political parties are naturally and rightly involved in representing the holders of conflicting views.

(b) *Complexity.* In the complex society of today opinion needs to be organised to be effective. Individual opinion cannot possess the width of specialised knowledge necessary for the management of modern administration, nor can it, except in rare cases, carry sufficient weight to command attention. Local political parties produce both the accumulation of the necessary specialised administrative techniques, and the weight of concerted opinion.

(c) *Increase in significance.* The involvement of the major political parties in local administration tends to increase the national significance of local government, and the key to the rejuvenation of local government probably rests in its acceptance as a projection, on an active local basis, of national policy. This widens the whole concept of the role and significance of local government.

4. Local advantages of local political parties.

(a) *Consistency of policy.* Effective local administration can only be obtained if there is a consistency of policy in the management of local affairs, and without some form of party discipline this would be very difficult to achieve. Party organisation ensures a definition of policy and its aims, and in doing so provides focal points for local affairs. The defining of matters of local importance educates the public, and ensures a greater interest in local affairs than could be obtained by the dissemination of a large variety of views on policy.

(b) *Hostility to individuals.* The existence of impersonal local political parties operates to transfer hostility which might be felt against individual members away from the members and towards the party.

(c) *Alternative unsatisfactory.* The only logical alternative to selection on party lines is that of selection according to personalities. While this was possible when local authorities represented small, comparatively homogeneous communities, it is not possible in the context of impersonal modern communities. It is surely more advantageous that local electors should be presented with a choice of understandable alternatives, rather than with the remote question of personalities, of whom they may have little knowledge. In addition a unified party has a greater chance of fulfilling its policies than have individuals whose policies may find little or no other support on the council.

5. General disadvantages of local political parties.

(a) *Scope.* In a large number of local authorities, particularly those of lower status, the scope for party divisions does not exist. The lack of powers requiring initiative rather than mere administrative work, and the overbearing authority of the central government, tends towards acceptance of the view that local authority politics is mere "playing at politics" and can do more harm than good.

(b) *Prior meetings.* Local decisions tend to be taken in prior party meetings rather than in open council meetings. The council may thus be in danger of becoming a mere rubber stamp of party decisions already taken. It also takes away from *public* view the discussion of matters which it is in the public interest to have discussed openly.

(c) *The whip.* The use of a whip system and its consequent party discipline stifles the initiative of individual councillors and discourages able individuals from undertaking council service.

(d) *Party ticket.* The need to represent an established party discourages and prevents independent members from standing for local elections.

(e) *Lack of importance.* It probably contributes little to local government, as general policy decisions are taken by the appropriate minister acting under statutory powers. But in certain issues scope does exist for party views, *e.g.* comprehensive education. However, the value of political alignment depends on the limited scope left to local authorities.

6. Unreality of local party divisions.

(a) *Lack of realism.* It may be contended that local political divisions involve illogical divisions of local authority business, and impose upon purely local issues the rather irrelevant categories of national problems.

(b) *Hampering efficiency.* They may hamper the working of effective local government by involving local authorities in disputes from policy standpoints over what are in fact largely matters of mere administration.

(c) *Lack of co-operation.* The system may be criticised on the grounds that it strikes at the roots of local government, as it tends to discourage the sharing of responsibility and the achievement of co-operation, by introducing strife where none should exist.

(d) *Clouding of issues.* Stress on party politics may operate to cloud the real issues involved.

(e) *Propaganda.* Local authorities provide platforms for political propaganda on issues which do not have the remotest relation to local government, *e.g.* the Liverpool Council's condemnation of the Suez operation of 1956. Such actions can only lead to a decrease in the respect for local authorities.

7. Conclusions. The more general the issues involved in local government, the greater the possibility of party politics. But, by predetermining issues on party lines, the open representative nature of the council is partly destroyed, and the initiative of the individual is reduced.

The basic difference between central and local politics is that in the former party organisation is all-important, as solidarity is required by the conventions of the constitution to ensure responsibility to the electorate. This does not apply to the same extent in local government.

8. The Maud Committee. The committee took the view that local politics were to be deplored where they produced irrelevant and sterile debate, or stifled discussion, or where they dictated the approach towards issues which were clearly non-political. However, it was felt that such divisions were likely to grow with reorganisation.

THE MACHINERY OF ELECTIONS

9. The right to vote. During the nineteenth century it was possible in some local authorities for an individual to have from one to six votes according to the amount he paid in local taxes. It was also possible to vote as an owner and as an occupier of property. These extra votes were abolished in 1870.

At the present day the law makes residence the sole test for voting in parliamentary elections. Local government still retains a form of duality by providing a system where an individual may be entitled to more than one vote, but can only use one vote at each election: *e.g.* if an individual had a residence qualification in one borough and owned a shop in another, he would be entitled to exercise a vote in each borough election, but could not vote twice in the county elections if both boroughs were within the same county.

10. Electoral areas. The following electoral areas and subdivisions exist:

(a) *Administrative counties* are divided into *electoral divisions*, with one councillor representing each division.

(b) *Boroughs and urban districts* are divided into *wards*, with three councillors representing each ward.

(c) *Rural districts* are divided into *parishes* or *groups of parishes* or *the ward of a parish*, and the number of councillors for each electoral area is fixed by the county council.

(d) *Parishes* are represented as electoral areas either by the *whole parish* or *wards of the parish*, and the number of councillors is fixed by the county council.

(e) *Rural boroughs* when created will either have the *whole borough* as their electoral area, or *wards of the borough*. The number of councillors will be fixed by the county council.

(f) *Greater London Council* is divided into its *parliamentary divisions*, and one councillor represents each division.

(g) *London boroughs* are divided into *wards*, with three councillors for each ward.

For voting convenience counties, boroughs and the London boroughs are generally divided into *polling districts*.

11. The franchise. By virtue of the *Representation of the People Act*, 1949, a person may vote at a local election if he satisfies all the following conditions:

(a) At the qualifying date he has property qualification based on residence, or on the occupation of property with an annual value of over £10 (or has a service qualification).

(b) He is a British subject of full age, and is not suffering from any legal incapacity.

NOTE: Legal incapacities involve:

(i) *Common law*. Idiots and persons of unsound mind are disqualified from voting.

(iii) *Statutes*. Persons convicted of treason or felony and punished with up to 12 months imprisonment are debarred from voting until they have served their sentence. (*Forfeiture Act*, 1870.)

Also persons guilty of corrupt or illegal practices are debarred from voting for five years. (*Representation of the People Act*, 1949.) Where illegal practices are involved, the disqualification is only effective in the local government area where such practices took place.

(c) He is included on the register of electors.

12. Register of electors. The compilation of the register is the duty of the registration officer, who is the clerk to the county council, and the clerk or town clerk in other areas.

This must be compiled on the basis of a sufficient local inquiry —usually house-to-house. Note that in cases where constituency boundaries and local government boundaries are not co-terminous, the registration officer will be appointed by the Secretary of State.

In all cases a new registration must be made each year.

13. Candidature. *See* V, **1, 2.**

14. Frequency of elections. The practice of holding annual elections in boroughs and district councils is open to a certain amount of criticism on the following grounds:

(*a*) *Interest.* Interest in local elections as represented by the percentage of the electorate going to the polls is already at an extremely low ebb. It is difficult to see how annual elections can do other than reduce the interest by increasing the large number of local elections.

(*b*) *Inconvenience.* Apart from the inconvenience of electoral organisation, difficulties are caused by the need to recast the membership of committees to meet changing membership, and by the time wasted in electioneering.

It is thus suggested that triennial elections on a compulsory basis would be desirable.

PROGRESS TEST 11

1. To what extent do party politics impinge upon local elections? **(1)**

2. What are the advantages and disadvantages of local political divisions? **(2–8)**

3. Who may vote at local elections? **(9, 11)**

4. What are the electoral areas? **(10)**

5. What comments may be made on the frequency of elections? **(14)**

CHAPTER XII

THE REFORM OF LOCAL GOVERNMENT

IS LOCAL GOVERNMENT STILL DESIRABLE?

1. Introduction. A pertinent and provocative comment has appeared in *The Times* which described local self-government "as a legacy of the nineteenth century interest in democratic forms. It is beginning to look as if confidence in it and the practice of it may prove to be a passing phase in British political evolution."

Before dealing with the detailed defects of local government and proposed structural and functional reforms, we must consider how it is that such comments come to be made about local government, when it is "the biggest business in Britain. It employs more than 1,800,000 persons . . . one-thirteenth of the working population. It spends an amount equal to one-eleventh of all domestic spending. It owns and manages one-quarter of the nation's homes; educates more than 7 million children; makes and maintains most of its roads; and administers a vast and growing complex of protective, welfare and amenity services" (*NALGO evidence to Royal Commission on Local Government*).

2. Reasons for low standing. Ignoring at this stage the functional and structural defects of local government, one must ask why such a vast organisation meets with public apathy, distrust and disrespect. It is suggested that this may be owing to the following reasons, given in **3** and **4** below.

3. Contrasted with central government.

(*a*) It is *overshadowed by the national government*. There is a general press, radio and television obsession with the affairs of the central government out of all proportion to its relative importance, with the result that there is a general ignorance of local government and a tendency to regard it as an extremely subsidiary form of government.

148

(b) In a *unitary state* local bodies must of necessity occupy a minor role, as the main powers of government are increasingly reserved to the central body, and all local powers stem from it.

(c) *Belief in central efficiency.* There seems to be a belief that matters must be administered more efficiently from the centre than at local level.

4. Other reasons.

(a) *Efficiency.* Though it is *non-profit making*, there is a tendency to judge it by business ideas of efficiency and inefficiency, and not to consider it in its social and public service role. This leads to unfair criticisms being made.

(b) *Quasi-judicial and restrictive character.* This tends to lead to hostility, reinforced by the number of controls which it has to impose as part of its functions. In many cases personal contact with a local authority is concerned with its controlling functions, *e.g.* planning restrictions are often seen in individual cases as petty and frustrating.

(c) *Official attitudes.* In a large number of cases the official attitude in dealing with new services has been to avoid giving them to local authorities. Also, since the War, the growing practice has been to transfer functions to larger authorities and to direct organs of the state.

(d) *Outdated formalities.* The pomp and ceremony associated with local government does not appeal to the public nowadays, and in fact may overshadow the practical aspects of its work.

5. Why retain local self-government?

Certain arguments in favour of local government are based on philosophical grounds, *e.g.* that it is the "seedbed of democracy," and are difficult to substantiate as they are rather vague. Neither can a functional division be made between the "local" and "national," as it has been seen that such a distinction is not really possible (*see* I, **4**).

Yet the centralist states of Eastern Europe have recognised that they need to inject some local autonomy, and that centralisation is not the complete answer. Thus the following arguments in favour of the continuance of local self-government may be advanced.

6. Reasons for retaining local self-government.

(a) *Resolving of competing claims.* It enables competing claims on resources and manpower to be decided at the point

F

of execution. Such claims will be resolved by elected members representing the interests of the consumers of the services, who will be able to take account of local needs and circumstances in deciding allocations.

(b) *Provision of pressure groups.* Local authorities provide powerful political pressure groups capable of tempering the power of the central government.

(c) *Central efficiency.* There is little definite evidence that the central government is in fact of necessity more efficient than local authorities; *e.g.* the hospital service has not been run more efficiently since its transfer to the central government.

(d) *Political interest.* It is thought that local self-government helps to sustain and increase an interest in politics. However, at present local authorities are not given enough discretion to take advantage of this, and their true role will have to be played within a reformed local government structure.

DEFECTS OF THE PRESENT SYSTEM

7. Main structural defects. The following structural defects exist in the present system:

(a) *Lack of logic.* There is an absence of logic in the area structure, with considerable variations within each titular category in such matters as size of area, population and financial resources (*see* III).

(b) *Town and country division.* The development of the system based on a rigid distinction between town and country is becoming more and more unrealistic at the present day, with the continued spread of the conurbations.

(c) *Effectiveness of county boroughs.* The abuse of the county borough idea when it was first applied has led to the existence of a large number of "all-purpose" authorities without the size to achieve maximum efficiency. As a result the county structure is unjustifiably broken up.

(d) *Administrative units too small.* The individual local government units are too small to play an effective part in strategic planning and national policy, or to reap the economies of large-scale organisation.

8. Other structural defects.

(a) *Distribution of functions.* Functions have been allocated to particular categories of local authorities without enough consideration of whether the individual authorities within each category are suited to the efficient carrying out of the particular function.

(b) *National issues.* It does not provide a suitable pattern for deciding such national issues as the location of industry, population changes and communications, and so the influence of local authorities in such matters is considerably reduced.

(c) *Rigidity of structure.* The tremendous changes in the nature and scope of the services administered by local authorities has resulted in a piecemeal allocation of functions. Local authorities have been structurally incapable of adaptation to the needs of new services, and to such factors as population growth and re-distribution.

(d) *Re-organisation.* Reforms, with the exception of Greater London, have to date been on a piecemeal and unplanned basis (*see* **16–18** below).

9. Constitutional defects. These have been dealt with in V above, and therefore need only be briefly stated as:

- (a) Inefficient use of the committee system.
- (b) Nineteenth century attitudes towards the relationship between members and officers.
- (c) Lack of a clear definition of the respective responsibilities of members and officers.
- (d) The aldermanic system.

10. Lack of local autonomy. The subject of central government control of local government has been dealt with in VII. It is therefore enough to say here that the overpowering control of the central government, emphasised through local financial dependence, has produced or contributed to the following defects of local government:

- (a) A poorer quality of members are attracted, owing to the lack of local powers of discretion and responsibilities.
- (b) A poorer quality of officer is attracted owing to the small amount of individual initiative he may be allowed.
- (c) A lack of interest on the part of the public and the press in the affairs of local authorities.

REGIONALISM

11. What is it? The most often suggested way of reforming the structure of local government has been that of regional local government, probably based on *city-regions.* This means re-establishing local government on a basis of wide regions centred upon important urban population areas. This will not necessarily involve the complete abolition of the present structure, but would lead to the main services requiring region-wide administration being dealt with by the regional authority, and lesser functions by enlarged local authorities, probably on a system similar to that adopted in Greater London, but covering a wider geographical area.

12. Advantages of wider regional local government areas.

(a) *Effective economic planning.* Large regional authorities would have at their disposal enough resources and powers to enable them to exert influence on the Government's economic planning. For this planning the principal agents at present are the regional planning boards set up in 1965 to study regional economic problems and report to the Department of Economic Affairs. They act in collaboration with local councils. Regional local authorities could assume this role, and, in addition to simplifying the administrative structure for planning, it would provide a democratic counter-weight to central economic planning.

(b) *Environmental planning.* Large regional authorities would be able to achieve environmental planning over an area as a whole and not on the present rather piecemeal scale. By assuming wide responsibility their powers would extend beyond mere planning as such, and would incorporate real powers for the development of their area.

(c) *Large-scale organisation.* Regional authorities would provide larger catchment areas for the services which need large-scale organisation to operate efficiently and economically. They would be able to use their resources economically by planning for the needs of a large area, *e.g.* in further education.

13. Other advantages of regional local government.

(a) *Members and staffs.* The increase in powers and responsibilities would attract a better class of officer and member, and would justify (because of the wider scope of administration) the appointment of highly specialised staff. It would also contribute to the more efficient use of manpower.

(b) *Training.* A large authority will be in a better position, both from a financial and a manpower point of view, to invest in training programmes.

(c) *Greater powers.* There would be less justification for the automatic vesting of new powers in the hands of government agencies, as the need for doing so would be met by the new authorities.

(*d*) *Capital*. Such authorities would be in a better position to raise capital in the open market, and would be in a stronger bargaining position as against the central government for the granting of loan sanction. They would possibly also reduce the need for the equalising element in central grants, and by their greater power would be able to counteract the policy-controlling powers of central financial aid.

14. Case against regional authorities.

(*a*) *Power*. It would be almost impossible to achieve a satisfactory balance of power between the central government and the regional authorities. The granting of too much power could lead to a weakening of the central authority, and result in the need to exercise strict control over the regions, thus not solving the problem of local independence. On the other hand to grant too little power would effectively question the whole justification of the existence of such bodies, unless they were confined to purely administrative and advisory roles.

(*b*) *Functions*. There are certain functions which cut across any possible local boundaries, *e.g.* location of industry, major traffic development, investment programmes and priorities. Such matters must be settled nationally, as they call for the resources and power of the central government. Thus it is difficult to attribute anything but an advisory role to the regions in major issues of this sort.

(*c*) *Unity of purpose*. It is likely that there will be internal disagreement between the various representations of areas within a region. It is difficult to imagine such bodies effectively taking decisions on the location of industry, slum clearance, etc. from a dispassionate point of view, or even reaching agreement on such matters. This lack of decision would call for the imposition of duties and the making of orders by the central government.

(*d*) *Remoteness*. Regional authorities could become too remote from the individual electors, and thus possibly increase frustration and fail to achieve a greater interest in local affairs.

NOTE: This could be balanced by the retaining of "local" units within the regional structure. The region would be responsible for the services which needed a wide area, and enlarged local units could be strengthened.

15. London government. The HMSO publication *Lessons of London Government Reform* comments that the clear statutory distinctions in the London area make for efficiency, and that the GLC has the merit of controlling functions where overall control is essential in a large city both for reasons of economy and efficiency, and for the dissemination of scientific and technical knowledge. The London boroughs also benefit from having wider powers and greater resources, which is resulting in the raising of standards.

REMEDYING OF DEFECTS

16. Early reforms. Reforms to date, with the exception of the Greater London area, have been extremely piecemeal and in fact almost non-existent. In 1926 the qualifying population figure for elevation to county borough status was raised from 50,000 to 75,000, and this status could only be achieved through a private Act of Parliament. There were no further applications until 1949–53, when several unsuccessful ones were made.

The *Local Government Act*, 1929, acting on the report of the *Onslow Commission*, resulted in *county reviews* during the 1930s, which reduced the number of districts from 1,606 to 1,048.

17. Local Government Boundary Commission, 1945. This was the first attempt to make a full-scale examination of the local government *structure* (*functions* being expressly excluded from its terms of reference).

NOTE: The *Reading Committee*, also set up in 1945 to examine London Government, was wound up a year later without making any recommendations.

(*a*) It made the point that it was impossible to separate territorial and functional considerations.

(*b*) It suggested the need for uniformity among the first-tier authorities, and recommended a population minimum for counties and county boroughs of 200,000. The result would be the creation of 67 new authorities, with only the twenty largest towns having county borough status. The remaining authorities would be organised on a tier basis in the same form as the existing structure.

(*c*) The majority of the existing county boroughs would become *most-purpose* authorities existing within the new county structure.

18. Effect of the boundary commission. The scheme found an almost complete absence of local authority and ministerial support, and in 1949 the commission was abolished without any of its suggestions obtaining statutory recognition.

19. White Papers. Tentative agreement was finally reached during the 1950s between the County Councils Association and the Association of Municipal Corporations, whose disagreement had been the stumbling block to any considerations of structural reform. The agreement was reached by the assurance of the Minister that no fundamental and drastic reforms were contemplated. The White Papers *Areas and Status of Local Authorities in England and Wales*, 1956 (Cmnd. 9831), and the *Functions of County Councils and County Districts in England and Wales*, 1957 (Cmnd. 161), laid down the principles for future reform which culminated in the Act of 1958.

20. The Local Government Act, 1958. Part II of the Act contained the following provisions for reviews of local government in England and Wales:

(*a*) *Two Local Government Commissions* were created, one for England and one for Wales.

(*b*) *Five special review areas* were established: Tyneside, South-east Lancashire, West Yorkshire, West Midlands and Merseyside.

(*c*) *The remainder* was divided into *general review areas* in which the commission was to make recommendations to secure "effective and convenient local government."

NOTE:

(*i*) *General review areas*. The commission is confined to first-tier authorities, and the review of districts was to be the function of the individual counties when their own areas were settled.

(*ii*) *Functions*. The commissions had no power to consider functions.

21. Powers of the commissions.

(*a*) *In all areas* the commissions could make recommendations involving:

(*i*) Alteration of county and county borough areas.

(*ii*) Constitution of new administrative counties.

(*iii*) Constitution of a new county borough by amalgamation of districts, elevation of status, or division of existing county boroughs and amalgamations of the parts.

    (*iv*) Abolition of counties and county boroughs and re-distribution to existing areas.

    (*v*) Conversion of a county borough into a non-county borough.

    (*vi*) Minor matters.

  (*b*) *In the special review areas*, in addition to any of the above matters the commission could propose:

    (*i*) Alteration of county district areas.

    (*ii*) Constitution of new county boroughs by amalgamation of existing areas.

    (*iii*) Constitution of new districts by the amalgamation of existing districts.

    (*iv*) Abolition of any urban and rural districts.

    (*v*) Conversion of urban into rural districts, and vice-versa.

22. Inquiry procedure. The commissions' power of review were further limited by the extremely complicated and dilatory review procedure. Basically this was as follows:

  (*a*) Written evidence from interested parties is taken.

  (*b*) Private consultations with such bodies are then held.

  (*c*) The commission then draws up proposals which are submitted by the Minister.

  (*d*) If local authorities involved raise objections a public local inquiry has to be held.

  (*e*) The report is finally submitted to Parliament.

23. Guiding factors. The commissions must also take into account in framing proposals such matters as:

  (*a*) Community of interest.

  (*b*) Expected economic development of the areas.

  (*c*) Physical features.

  (*d*) Record of administration.

  (*e*) The size and shape of the proposed areas.

  (*f*) The wishes of the inhabitants. This has generally been interpreted as the wishes of the local authority, and has proved a considerable obstacle to any sweeping proposals.

24. Special review area proposals.

  (*a*) *West Midlands*. The Black Country area has been reorganised into six county boroughs as from 1964. The principal defect of the report was that it failed to take the step of creating a new authority for the whole conurbation of the Birmingham area, which has shown a sixfold increase since its establishment in 1889 as a county borough.

(b) *West Yorkshire.* Little or nothing has been done in this area, despite the need for a new county authority to cover the whole area. The report of the Commission on this area was particularly piecemeal.

(c) *Tyneside.* The commission made comprehensive suggestions involving the creation of a new "Tyneside County Council," and the creation of four most-purpose authorities out of the existing county boroughs of Newcastle, Gateshead, Tynemouth and South Shields, which would administer the remaining functions and replace the existing patchwork of local authorities. The Minister rejected the proposals, and proposed instead the creation of a new county borough for Tyneside.

(d) *Merseyside.* The commission has recommended the establishment of a joint planning board for Merseyside with the existing structure otherwise unchanged.

(e) *South-east Lancashire.* The commission proposed that there should be a continuous county for the area, comprising 500 square miles and drawing population from the counties of Lancashire and Cheshire. At the second tier nine "most-purpose" authorities should be formed by amalgamations.

25. General review areas.

(a) *West Midlands.* The downgrading of two county boroughs was proposed, though the proposal to downgrade Burton-on-Trent was rejected, and the proposal to downgrade Worcester has proved legally abortive.

(b) *East Midlands.* The proposals here that have been accepted involved the amalgamation of Huntingdon and the Soke of Peterborough; Cambridge and the Isle of Ely; and the raising of Luton to county borough status. The amalgamation of Rutland with Leicestershire has been amazingly and illogically rejected. In addition the areas of Leicester and Northampton county boroughs were recommended for extension, and both proposals were accepted.

(c) *Wales.* The Welsh commission proposals were generally more radical than the English commission, but with the exception of certain rather unimportant county borough proposals they were scrapped *en bloc* in the face of their considerable political unpopularity.

(d) *South-western area.* No county alterations were proposed, and the principle recommendation involved the creation of a new Torbay County Borough.

(e) *North-eastern general review area.* This covered Northumberland and Durham and the North Riding of Yorkshire, excluding the special review areas. The main proposals concerned boundary extensions and the amalgamation of the Hartlepools into a single county borough.

(f) *Yorkshire and North Midlands.* Very limited boundary changes were proposed.

(g) *Lincolnshire and East Anglia.* The proposals for the area, which were in themselves extremely insignificant, were generally rejected by the Minister.

(h) *South-east.* These had not been made by 1965 when the commission suspended its own activities.

26. Appraisal of the commissions. The Royal Commissions are yet another ineffective episode in the history of local government reform. In fairness the Royal Commissions themselves are not entirely to be blamed, as they were hampered in the following ways:

(a) Inability to consider functional defects.
(b) Local authority hostility, often on fatuous and deliberately obstructive grounds.
(c) A dilatory form of procedure.
(d) Continual and disheartening lack of ministerial support and sympathy.

27. Criticisms of the commissions. In addition to the points mentioned above, the commissions may be criticised on the following grounds:

(a) They made no general attack on structure, and were concerned in many cases with piecemeal alterations and patching up of the existing system. It must be added, however, that sweeping proposals would have stood little chance of approval, but they would have accentuated the true needs of the commissions.

(b) They did not use research staffs to find out the real "wishes of the inhabitants," which would probably have been more helpful than many of the local authorities' suggestions, and perhaps more impartial.

THE FUTURE

28. Purpose of the commissions. When the Local Government Commissions were established in 1958, their terms of reference presupposed that the structure of local government needed only a minor and not a drastic overhaul. Sir Keith

Joseph stated that "reform along regionalist lines was both unnecessary and wrongheaded."

29. Changing government attitude. In *April 1965* the Minister, Mr. Crossman, stated that "all we can do, and all I shall work for is a better balance *within the existing system*, within the existing structure of county and borough, within the existing balance of central and local government. To plan for anything else is to mistake a pipe-dream for reality." His only criticisms seemed to be of a lack of co-ordination in the planning functions.

In *September 1965* he made a complete about-face in his attitude, when he stated that "the whole structure of local government is archaic and out of date. The counties and county boroughs as at present constituted are archaic institutions whose size and structure make them ill-adapted to fulfil the important functions with which they are charged." He commented of the commissions that "their terms of reference are too narrow," and "they have done their best on the Procrustean bed on which they were laid by Act of Parliament."

30. New beliefs. The Government adopted the attitude that there were two main problems:

   (*a*) There was no relation between size and function in local government.
   (*b*) The need is to resolve the conflict between local democracy, which is inherently small, and efficiency, which is sometimes on a large scale.

31. The new commission. The Royal Commissions saw no alternative but to wind up, in the light of their narrow terms of reference and the new government policy. The rejection of the special Tyneside review was the last straw, and in December 1965 the remaining English commission came to an end without even informing the Government of its intention.

In *February 1966* the old commission was formally wound up, and a new Royal Commission appointed to cover England and Scotland, Wales being excluded because of the advanced stage of Welsh reform. The commission has wider terms of reference and may "consider the structure of local government outside London in relation to its existing functions and make recommendations for authorities and boundaries, and for functions and their division, showing regard to the size and character of the areas in which these can be most effectively exercised and the need to sustain a viable system of local self-government." It may also consider regional proposals and the relations between central and local government.

32. Conclusion. The report of the commission is expected in 1969, but by the time it has been debated and objections heard, it is doubtful whether any statutory steps can be taken during the life of the present Government.

PROGRESS TEST 12

1. Is local government still desirable? **(1, 5, 6)**

2. Why is local government held in low esteem at the present day? **(2–4)**

3. What are the structural defects of the local government system? **(7, 8)**

4. What are its principal constitutional defects? **(9)**

5. What is the effect of the lack of local autonomy? **(10)**

6. What is "regionalism"? **(11)**

7. What are the advantages and the disadvantages of a regional system of local government? **(12–14)**

8. What reforms of the local government structure had taken place before the *Local Government Act, 1958*? **(16–19)**

9. What were the provisions of the *Local Government Act, 1958,* in the field of reform? **(20–23)**

10. What proposals were made by the Local Government Commission for the special review areas? **(24)**

11. Were any significant proposals made for the general review areas? **(25)**

12. What change in government attitude led to the terminating of the English commission? **(28–30)**

13. What are the terms of reference of the 1966 commission? **(31)**

CHAPTER XIII

COMPARATIVE SYSTEMS OF LOCAL GOVERNMENT

THE UNITED STATES OF AMERICA

1. Structure. The principal feature of local government in the USA is the wide variety of systems prevailing in individual States, and the large degree of freedom of the local units.

(*a*) *Constitutional status.* Local government organisation is the responsibility of the individual State government, and the degree of independence of local units is defined in State statutes and in individual charters of incorporation.

(*b*) *Home Rule charters.* Twenty-six States have adopted "Home Rule charters" which, when granted by the State legislature, allow cities to draft their own charters by local convention, with (or sometimes without) State ratification.

(*c*) *Special authorities.* There is a much greater tendency in the USA towards a proliferation of *ad hoc* authorities than there is in England, with the result that it is possible for a citizen to be affected by seven or eight different authorities operating in his area. There is a general absence of comprehensive areas.

(*d*) *Area structure.* This varies widely according to the pattern and traditions of historic settlements. In 1960 there were 3,000 or more counties and parishes with a population average of 45,000. Resistance to the consolidation of counties has been strong.

(*e*) *The city.* This is part of a county, but is in direct relations with the State government, and is the area of US local government showing the greatest integration of functions.

2. Finance. Local units have much more liberal financial powers and in particular:

(*a*) *Loan sanction* is usually not required, subject to limitations on total indebtedness.

(*b*) A greater variety of local sources of revenue is available (*see* IX, 51).

(*c*) *The proportion of grants* is much smaller than in the UK, though there is a tendency towards an increase in recent years.

3. Organisation. The principal forms of local organisation are:

   (a) *The town meeting.* A meeting of taxpayers to settle the main lines of policy, to choose officials, accept the budget, to control administration, etc. At present this is of decreasing importance and is practicable only in small areas.

   (b) *The commission system.* Administration by a small number of individuals elected as departmental heads, and forming the government of the city. This method is declining.

   (c) *Council and mayor system.* This system involves a separation of functions between an elected legislative council and an elected mayor as chief executive.

   (d) *City-manager.* (*See* V, **38–41**.)

4. Central control. The need to obtain sanction for administrative policies is rare, and is limited principally to public works schemes, and occasionally to highways, education and hospitals assisted by the State. The submission of reports is limited to the above matters, and there is a general absence of external compulsory audit. Similarly inspection is limited and there is no control of officials.

It would be generally correct to assume that this absence of control stems partly from the much greater financial independence of local authorities in the USA.

NOTE: The principal external control is *judicial control.*

FRANCE

5. Constitutional setting. French local government structure is highly centralised and has strong hierarchical leanings, with a percolation of control from the central government down to the smallest authorities.

   (a) *Areas.* French local government is divided in descending order of importance into *départements, arrondissements, cantons,* and *communes.* The *départements* and the *communes* are the true local government areas, the others being local administrative, electoral and gendarmerie units.

   The average population of *départements* is 500,000 and the *communes* vary from the smallest village up to Paris, though approximately two-thirds have a population of under 1,000. Powers and control vary according to size.

   (b) *Powers.* General competence powers exist, though these are subject to strong judicial control and administrative checking. In addition *obligatory* functions are placed on local authorities amounting to anything up to 80 per cent of functions measured in terms of revenue.

(c) *Organisation.* A centrally appointed *préfet* effectively regulates the *département* council, and in the *commune* the *maire* works in conjunction with a centrally appointed *secrétaire-général.*

A small standing committee of the council, the *Commission Départementale*, controls in co-operation with the *préfet* and is served by *adjoints* who supervise various departments of the council.

6. Finance. The budget is subject to superior authorisation by the *maire*, and the *préfet* may require it to balance and may write in mandatory expenditures, while rejecting discretionary matters.

7. Central control. The rural basis of French local government, together with political fears and instability, has resulted in stringent central control. This operates through vigilance on a hierarchical basis, government intervention and the control of administrative schemes. It is strengthened by official auditing of local accounts.

THE COMMONWEALTH

8. General pattern. As a general rule the older states of the Commonwealth, Australia, New Zealand and Canada, are mainly based on the English pattern. However, control by the individual State of its local authorities in Canada and Australia has resulted in a variety of systems.

Canada is generally divided into cities, towns or counties, though the more remote rural areas are generally controlled by the Government of the Province. An important feature of Canadian local government has been the adoption of the city manager system in Halifax, St. John, Victoria and most of the principal cities of Quebec. The *main revenues* are taxes on real property, sales taxes, poll taxes and business taxes, supplemented by large grants from the central government. Education is generally administered by separate school boards.

Australia, with its urban and rural councils, and *New Zealand* substantially follow the English pattern.

MISCELLANEOUS FACTORS

9. The Maud Committee. This made certain observations about the systems of local government in England and Wales and those in certain foreign countries; in particular it drew attention to the following:

(a) *Finance.* A close connection is revealed between freedom from central control and the possession of adequate local resources. The percentage of grants as part of local income is approximately 35 per cent in the USA, and the same in Sweden, while increasing to 100 per cent in the Netherlands. The greater the degree of financial dependence, the greater the degree of central control following in its wake, appears to be a reasonable assumption.

(b) *Size of authorities.* Local councils in England and Wales are considerably greater in number than their foreign counterparts.

(c) *Party politics.* There is very little on a local level in the USA, though it is much more prominent in Europe and particularly so in England and Wales.

(d) *Numbers voting.* Compared with a sample of foreign countries, the percentage of the electorate actually voting in England and Wales is extremely low.

(e) *Powers.* A greater degree of autonomy exists in Sweden, Holland and Germany, which is accentuated by local authorities having general competence powers. In the USA local authorities are regarded as participants in federal programmes rather than as mere agencies, as is the British tendency.

(f) *Officers.* There is a greater tendency abroad to delegate effective executive powers to officers, and thus there is a clearer definition of the responsibilities of the executive and legislative sides of local authority work.

10. Relevance of comparative studies. It is difficult to draw any absolute conclusions from a study of foreign systems without making due allowance for historical, social, political, geographical and other factors which have influenced them. It is suggested however that the following conclusions could be drawn:

(a) Greater freedom from control and of financial resources makes for a greater interest in local government.

(b) English local government is still suffering from a Victorian outlook in its inability to allow enough discretion to the paid officers.

(c) There is a need to strengthen local finances if local government in the true sense is to be strengthened.

(d) Local government abroad should be the subject of a more searching examination, especially the systems less affected by "tradition and local pride," in order to see what modernising features could usefully be imported into the English system.

PROGRESS TEST 13

1. Outline the local government system of the USA.   **(1–4)**
2. Outline the significant features of the French system.   **(5–7)**
3. What significant comments did the Maud Committee make on foreign systems of local government?   **(9)**
4. What use is a comparative study of local government?   **(10)**

CHAPTER XIV

THE ROYAL COMMISSION ON LOCAL GOVERNMENT

BACKGROUND TO THE REPORT

1. Introduction. The reform of the structure of local government up to the winding up of the previous Royal Commission and the appointment of the Redcliffe-Maud Commission in 1966 has been dealt with in XII. That chapter also dealt with the arguments for and against regionalism (*see* XII, **11–14**).

NOTE: In view of the important report of Mr. Derek Senior dissenting from the recommendations of the Redcliffe-Maud Commission, the concept of the city-region is more fully dealt with in this chapter (*see* **20–22** below).

2. The debate within the Commission. The intra-commission debate has been largely concerned with the business of finding a workable compromise, which would ensure that the re-organisation of local government would not mean that the interests of each local authority were submerged in the interests of the overall planning of local government and the administration of large and expensive local services.

The weight of evidence to the Commission showed that many authorities are too small and too restricted geographically to afford and provide good services.   This led to a polarising within the Commission of two principal alternatives:

(*a*) *Regionalism.* A few large top-tier authorities to take over some of both central and local government functions, while a second tier of authorities with populations ranging from 300,000 to 1 million would administer some of the existing local authority services.

(*b*) *The city-region.* The creation of 40 or more city-regions, or extended counties, with smaller second-tier authorities under them.   The 8 regional economic planning councils could be strengthened to form a first super-tier. The division of functions would be similar to that at present existing, but the second tier would be strengthened by the amalgamation of existing units.

3. Witnesses before the Commission. The following is a selection of the evidence given by some of the more important witnesses heard by the Commission:

(a) *The Local Authority Associations.* A remarkable degree of acceptance of the need for change in the local government structure was found in the evidence given to the Commission by the various associations representing local authorities. The principal associations, including the important County Councils Association, have supported the city-region approach. The C.C.A. was strongly anti-regionalist, believing it to be incompatible with true local government. Instead it suggested 40 to 50 modified counties swallowing up the existing county boroughs and following the existing county lines. The second tier should be enlarged urban and rural councils, with the division of powers similar to that existing at present.

The Association of Municipal Corporations wanted more city-regions (up to 100) which should be most-purpose authorities under provincial authorities, and with an emphasis on preserving "the local in local government."

The Rural District Councils Association warned the Commission that strong personal local links are the best basis on which to organise local government. This argument, however, has carried little weight with the Commission.

(b) *The Confederation of British Industries.* The C.B.I. suggested a two-tier system. The first tier to replace the existing counties and county boroughs and to cover larger areas. These regional authorities would be supported by district authorities, formed by the amalgamation of existing authorities.

(c) *N.A.L.G.O.* Favour was shown for the provincial approach, and 10 regional authorities were suggested plus a compromise of 120 to 150 most-purpose authorities.

(d) *The National Union of Teachers.* The N.U.T. warned the Commission against large amalgamations of the existing authorities, unless specific democratic safeguards were built into the revised system.

(e) *The Ministry of Housing and Local Government.* The Ministry was strongly in favour of the city-region approach.

PRINCIPLES GUIDING THE COMMISSION

4. The existing defects. The Commission listed the following faults in the present local government system:

(a) *Pattern.* Local council areas do not fit the pattern of life and work in modern England. This gap would widen as social, economic and technological change quickened.

(b) *Competition.* With county and district councils running services in competition, the proper planning of development and transport is impossible. In addition there exists an inbuilt hostility between town and country, which has made it difficult to decide controversial questions purely on their merits.

(c) *Complications.* With urban areas existing like islands in the counties, services which should be in the hands of one authority are split among several, complicating the work of meeting the needs of families and individuals.

(d) *Size.* Many local councils are too small in size and revenue, and are consequently starved of highly-specialised manpower and sophisticated technical equipment.

5. Failings in local government relations with the public and with the national government.

(a) *Ineffectiveness.* The complex and often irrelevant machinery of local government leads to ineffectiveness in dealing with personal problems and a sense of frustration among councillors and officers.

(b) *Lack of confidence.* Parliament and the central government doubt the ability of local governors, within the straitjacket of the present system to run local affairs.

(c) *Lack of unification.* The failure of local government to act as a single body *vis-à-vis* the central government arises from the multiplicity of types of authority and their representative bodies.

6. Principles behind the report of the Commission. The Commission based its conclusions on the following principles:

(a) *Defining of local government areas.* Local authority areas must be so defined that they enable citizens and their elected representatives to have a sense of common purpose.

(b) *Interdependence of town and country.*

(c) *Physical environment.* In each part of the county, all services concerned with the physical environment, *i.e.* planning, transport and major development, must be in the hands of one authority, and areas must be sufficiently large to enable these authorities to meet the pressing land needs of the growing population.

(d) *Personal services.* All personal services being closely linked in operation and effect must also be in the hands of one authority (as strongly recommended by the Seebohm Committee).

(e) *Concentration of authority.* Because they are inter-related and influence each other, both environmental and personal services should be in the hands of one authority.

(*f*) *Size.* Authorities must be bigger than county boroughs are at present, if they are to command the resources and skilled manpower which they need to provide services with maximum efficiency.

(*g*) *Minimum population.* The size of authorities must vary over a wide range if areas are to match patterns of population. However a minimum population is necessary, and the Commission concludes that this should be in the region of 250,000.

(*h*) *Maximum size.* At the other end of the scale authorities must not be so large in terms of population that organisation of their business becomes difficult, and the elected representatives cannot keep in touch with the people affected by their policies. This applies especially in the personal services. A maximum of one million is thought suitable, though much will depend on the social and geographical characteristics of each area.

(*i*) *Need for divisions.* Where the area required for planning and other environmental services contains too large a population for the purposes of the personal services, a single authority for all services is not appropriate. Therefore in a limited number of cases there is a need for division.

(*j*) *Tradition.* The new local government pattern should so far as practicable stem from the existing one. Wherever the case for change is in doubt, the common interests, traditions and loyalties inherent in the present pattern, and the strength of existing services as going concerns, should be respected.

THE PROPOSED NEW STRUCTURE

7. The areas.

(*a*) *Provincial level.* Eight provincial councils, indirectly elected to set the strategic framework for the operational authorities, replacing the present regional economic planning councils. They would collaborate with the central government in the economic and social development of each province. A possible increase in their power is envisaged following the Crowther Report on constitutional reform, but until then they will be responsible for the regional plan and will be concerned with planning, research and co-ordination. In addition they will have oversight to prevent coalescence of urban areas, and to regulate overspill.

(*b*) *Operational level.* Fifty-eight elected "unitary" authorities singly responsible for all services. However in three new metropolitan areas, Merseyside, SELNEC (S.E. Lancs, N.E. and Central Cheshire) and the West Midlands, there would be a division of functions between the three metropolitan authorities and the twenty District Councils (*see* **17–18** below). These authorities stem from the view of the Commission that the greatest strength of the present system is that of county boroughs with strong co-ordinated leadership.

(*c*) *Local level.* To represent communities, an elected council for each present county borough, borough and urban district, and for each parish in which there is now a parish council.

8. Principles of the new structure.

(*a*) England (outside London) is to be divided into 61 local government areas, each covering both town and country.

(*b*) In 58 a single authority is to be responsible for all services. In the specific circumstances of three metropolitan areas a division of responsibility is suggested.

(*c*) The 61 new authorities are to be grouped, together with Greater London, in 8 provinces each with a provincial council.

(*d*) Provincial councils are to be elected by the authorities for the unitary and metropolitan areas (and Greater London authorities), but including also co-opted members.

(*e*) The key function of the provinces would be to settle the provincial strategy, and the planning framework within which the main authorities will operate.

(*f*) The province will collaborate with the government in the economic and social development of the province. Provinces will also play a part in the future adaptation of local government to the changing needs, ways of life, and movement that time and technical progress will bring.

(*g*) Within the 58 unitary authorities, and, whenever they are wanted, within the metropolitan areas, local councils should be elected to represent and communicate the wishes of cities, towns and villages in all matters of special concern to the inhabitants.

(*h*) The only *duty* of the local council would be to represent local opinion, but it would have the right to be consulted on matters of special concern, and the *power* to do for the local community a number of things best done locally, including the opportunity to play a part in some of the main local government services on a scale appropriate to its resources, and subject to the agreement of the main authority.

GEOGRAPHICAL DIVISIONS

9. The South-West. This will consist of 8 new unitary authorities to take over from the existing 192. The province will stretch north to the Cotswolds, west to the Scilly Isles, and east to the New Forest. The authorities will range in size from Bristol and Bath, with one million population, to Plymouth, which will be greatly enlarged to take in 314,000. Other important authorities will be Exeter and Devon (taking in Torbay), and Bournemouth and Dorset.

10. The North-West. This stretches from Carlisle in the north to Chester in the south. It will include 7 unitary authorities and 2 metropolitan areas at Liverpool and Manchester, replacing the existing 201 authorities.

The SELNEC metropolis will have a population of 3·2 million, with 9 district councils ranging from Manchester with 979,000 to Warrington with 176,000.

The Merseyside metropolis will have 4 district councils, *i.e.* Southport–Crosby (298,000); Liverpool (936,000); St. Helens–Widnes (274,000); and South Merseyside (555,000).

Blackburn, Preston, Blackpool and Burnley will be centres of new unitary authorities. Westmorland is divided between Cumberland and North Westmorland, and a further authority will cover the area surrounding Morecambe Bay.

11. The West Midlands. Birmingham and the Black Country form a new metropolitan area running from Stafford to Redditch with a population of 3 million. There will be 7 metropolitan area districts ranging from 200,000 to 1,314,000 and including Solihull, Meriden and Sutton Coldfield.

The metropolitan area will be surrounded by 4 new unitary authorities based on Shropshire–Warwickshire, Worcestershire–Herefordshire, and parts of Staffordshire and Cheshire.

12. Yorkshire. The Yorkshire province will have 10 unitary authorities compared with the existing 152, and will extend from Scarborough to Sheffield and from Grimsby to Aysgarth. There will be a population of 4·8 million.

The North Riding remains substantially intact, but the West Riding is divided into two linear areas stretching north from Bradford and from Leeds. The Sheffield and South Yorkshire authority will have a population of over one million and will take in Barnsley, Rotherham, Penistone and part of the Peak National Park. A specific function of the regional council will be the development of Humberside, which is divided into two authorities.

13. The North-East. There will be 5 unitary authorities, the largest of which will embrace Tyneside (population of over one million). Teesside is expanded to include Hartlepool and most of the North Yorkshire National Park. The provincial council is to be specially responsible for ensuring a fair allocation of resources between Tyneside, Teesside, the sparsely populated rural areas and the declining areas of County Durham.

A notable overall narrowing of rateable value per head is achieved, *i.e.* from £30 8*s.* in Sunderland and East Durham to £43 7*s.* in Teesside.

14. The East Midlands. There will be 4 unitary authorities in a province of 3 million. The authorities will be based on Derby and Derbyshire; Nottingham and Nottinghamshire; Leicester and Leicestershire; and Lincoln and Lincolnshire. Populations will range from 398,000 to 997,000.

The special responsibility of the provincial council will be to oversee the incipient conurbation in the Derby, Nottingham and Leicester triangle.

15. East Anglia. The province divides conveniently into 4 new unitary authorities consisting of Peterborough, Norfolk, Cambridgeshire, and Ipswich, and their hinterlands. These in fact are admirable city-region areas.

16. The South-East. This is the largest province, with 17 new all-purpose authorities and including the Greater London Area. It will extend north to take in the London overspill areas of Corby and Northamptonshire. The population of the province will be 17 million, including 7·7 million in Greater London.

Surrey will be divided into East and West Surrey. Hertfordshire will become East Herts; and Luton and West Herts. Bedfordshire will be merged with North Bucks. Kent is divided into West Kent; and Canterbury and East Kent. Hampshire is divided in two—Southampton and South Hants; and Portsmouth, South-East Hants and the Isle of Wight. Sussex is divided into three—West Sussex; Brighton and Mid-Sussex; and East Sussex.

Populations range from 327,000 (East Sussex) to 872,000 (West Kent).

METROPOLITAN AREAS

17. The metropolitan authority. This will be responsible for the following matters:

(a) *Planning transport intelligence.*

(b) *Housing.* Metropolitan housing policy, building in the interest of the metropolis as a whole, building to ensure the fulfilment of planning policies, policy for the selection of tenants, metropolitan rent policy.

(c) *Public health.* Water supply, main sewerage, sewage disposal, refuse disposal, clean air.

(d) *The Arts.* Metropolitan museums, galleries, promoting the arts, entertainments, sports, parks and recreation grounds.

(e) *Police, fire and ambulance services.*

(f) *Co-ordination of investment.*

18. Metropolitan district councils. These will deal with education; libraries; youth employment; personal social services; personal health services; housing (within the framework of metropolitan policy), *i.e.* building in accordance with metropolitan policy, housing management and all other housing matters.

Local sewers and drains; coast protection; clean air enforcement; museums, galleries, etc., in the interests of individual districts; food and drugs; weights and measures; consumer protection; Shops Acts; licensing of places of public entertainment; registration of births, deaths and marriages; and rating.

ADVANTAGES OF THE NEW SYSTEM

19. The Commission's views.

(a) *Unification.* Planning and transport problems and future development can be tackled as a whole, and not on a piecemeal basis through a large number of different authorities.

(b) *Education.* Outside the universities, education would be under the control of the unitary authority, and thus 78 authorities will replace the existing 280.

(c) *Family service.* The way is opened for a complete family service, including the care of the homeless, of handicapped children, of the mentally handicapped, etc., all linked and related to education, health and housing. This will be of particular advantage if, as recommended by the Commission, the administration of the National Health Service is transferred to the unitary authorities.

(*d*) *Housing.* House building and management will be in the hands of 81 authorities instead of the present number of more than 1,000. Building will thus be encouraged because larger and more extended orders could be placed. It will also facilitate mobility of tenants.

(*e*) *Manpower.* Better and more economic use of highly qualified, and therefore scarce, manpower can be made.

(*f*) *Shift of power.* The new structure will result in a shift of power and responsibility from the central government to strengthened local councils. This will also involve a better and more meaningful dialogue between the central and local government. (Lord Redcliffe-Maud has commented in a television interview, given since the Commission's report, that the central government will be only too willing to effect such a transfer of responsibility.)

(*g*) *Finance.* It will be possible to liberate local authorities from their present excessive dependence on funds from Whitehall, by the transference of sources of revenue from the central to the local government.

NOTE: All this, Redcliffe-Maud believes, would encourage people to take a greater active interest in local government.

DISSENT

20. The memorandum of dissent. The memorandum prepared by one Commission member, Mr. Derek Senior, is fundamentally opposed to the views of the Commission, and was not accepted by the other members. However, it will undoubtedly act as a potent catalyst to produce debate before the recommendations of the Commission are accepted.

21. The arguments of Senior.

(*a*) He argues that the main authorities proposed by the Commission are inappropriate in most situations.

(*b*) They are too small to be effective planning authorities, and too large to be accessible administrators of the personal social services.

(*c*) The Achievement of unitary authorities, although a worthwhile objective, has been sought at the cost of all else.

(*d*) A two-tier system would have worked better in more situations. The upper tier would control planning, transport, investment, police and education, with the lower tier controlling personal service functions, *i.e.* health, welfare, child care and housing management.

(e) The Commission should have been guided primarily by social geography. Where people live and work and what area they function in would provide a guide line. This would involve the creation of larger units than the Commission favours, and would produce 35 "regional development authorities," beneath which he recommends 148 second-tier authorities.

(f) The unitary principle simply does not fit the geography of England. It involves unnatural marriages, and as examples of this he cites Maidstone and Tunbridge Wells, Durham and Darlington, and Aylesbury and High Wycombe. He argues that the areas are not merely lacking in coherence but are positively fissile.

(g) He asks why the Commission accepts the need for two levels of authority in certain areas, but does not consider that conurbations, such as Newcastle, Leeds, Sheffield, Nottingham, Southampton, Bristol and Preston, warrant dual authorities.

NOTE: It may be pointed out in defence of the Commission that it only resorted to the metropolitan principle in extreme cases, and that the arguments based on the urban sprawl and population of Birmingham, Liverpool and Manchester do not apply on such a scale to the examples cited by Mr. Senior.

(h) He also criticises the majority for sticking where possible to existing administrative boundaries, rather than following the traffic "watersheds" between the service areas of the unitary authorities.

(i) He concludes that the majority seek to gain administrative convenience during the period of transition, but at the cost of the future coherence (and efficiency) of the units.

FURTHER POINTS

22. Views on the city-region.

(a) The city-region has value, the Commission considers, because it takes account of the fact that people are more mobile now than they were before.

(b) Witnesses have been greatly at variance as to the appropriate number of city-regions, thus suggesting to the Commission that it was not an idea that could be applied uniformly all over England. It also does not seem to fit the facts in certain parts of the country. It provides a clue to structural organisation in a number of areas, particularly around the great concentrations of Birmingham, Liverpool and Manchester, and also in parts where a big town is the natural centre for a wide area of surrounding countryside and smaller towns, e.g. in East

Anglia and Cambridgeshire. But in the South-West it would mean artificially contrived areas, and in the South-East any natural local centre which may exist is overshadowed by London (particularly is this so in the commuter belt).

(c) Many city-regions would be so large as to need a second operational tier of authorities, if local government is not to be too remote for effective contact between the elected representatives and the people. In addition many second-tier authorities would be too small to find the resources necessary for the main services. There would also be an undesirable splitting of responsibility for the personal services.

23. Other recommendations.

(a) *Membership*. There should be single-member constituencies for both main and local authorities, with a maximum of 75 elected members in the unitary authorities and 50 on the local councils. Each provincial council would be elected by the authority for the unitary and metropolitan authority plus 20–25 per cent co-opted members.

(b) *Finance*. The reorganisation should be the occasion for a fundamental rethinking of the present shortcomings of the system of local taxation. The Government should allow other local taxes in order to increase local autonomy, *e.g.* motor vehicle licence revenue should be transferred to the local authorities. Investment and borrowing powers for local government should be facilitated.

(c) *Capital expenditure*. This needs to be planned as a rolling programme stretching 5 years ahead. Each authority is to have a discretionary margin within a comprehensive investment programme for its area.

(d) *Revision*. The areas decided upon for the main authorities should be established for 5 years, and changes thereafter should be initiated by the central government or proposed by the provincial council.

(e) *Aldermen*. The office of alderman is to be abolished.

(f) *Priorities*. Each unitary authority to have a central committee to guide strategy and to fix priorities.

(g) *Division of responsibility*. The roles of councillor and officer are to be clarified, with the latter solely responsible for day-to-day administration.

CONCLUSIONS

24. The need for reform. The wide issues involved in the need for reform may be gathered from the following expressions of opinion:

(a) "*Democracy in the balance.*" Professor D. V. Donnison writing in the *Guardian* (12 June 1969) pointed out that the next twenty years are crucial for the social welfare in our industrial society, in determining whether society will disintegrate into affluent suburban majorities living round the fringe of deprived minorities. The need for drastic action in housing, education, urban renewal and the quality of the social services is stressed in the reports of Newsom, Milner Holland, Plowden and Seebohm, but action itself depends on effective local government. He considers that the evidence before the Commission shows that in its present form local government could not cope; in particular he points to Appendix 5 (continued growth in number of children and old people), Appendix 6 (impossibility of maintaining present growth in local expenditure) and Chapter III (the failure of major urban authorities to find space to house 'their people at tolerable standards). He concludes that on strictly administrative grounds the Commission is unassailable in general terms.

(b) *The Commission's summing up.* The Commission points out that many existing social defects contrast strongly with people's rising expectations, and call urgently for replacement. In modern conditions there is expansion of industrial organisation, financial needs and demand for services, and in the face of the government's increasing power there must be a corresponding increase in the effectiveness of local government. If this does not occur, local government will be swamped by the pressures and powers of the central authority, and a highly centralised form of government will result. It concludes that "to most people in England this is unacceptable, but if there is no counterpoise it must come."

25. Arguments for the recommendations. These are largely given above (*see* 19) and as notes to 26 and 27 below. However, the following points may also be mentioned:

(a) The undeniable need for reform of some sort.

(b) The danger of the atrophy of local government.

(c) The need for the unification of services which are interrelated.

(d) The importance of strengthening local powers at the critical unitary level.

(*e*) The recognition of the integrated nature of services and that such services can only be operated with maximum efficiency and economy as a single unit. Particularly on the personal service side the unitary structure will enable education, social services, housing, etc. to be integrated within areas small enough for maintaining democratic contact.

(*f*) The creation of provincial councils will strengthen economic planning and give real power over development.

26. Main disadvantages of the recommendations.

(*a*) *Is bigger better?* The Commission, despite persuasive subjective evidence on the advantages of size, is able to offer no *objective* evidence for this. In addition the optimum level for one service may not be the optimum for another. Size does create certain problems while solving others, *e.g.* the New York school system is in danger of breaking up, and increasing demands for "neighbourhood control" are being made.

NOTE: The population criteria for the new authorities fall in with the recommendations of Seebohm on the personal social services and the views of the Department of Education and Science upon education. It must be observed that any individual figure which the Commission fixed could be criticised, but it appears that the figures do meet the needs of the majority of services, particularly the vital environmental services.

(*b*) *"Grass Roots" level.* A major criticism that can, and undoubtedly will, be levelled at the Commission is its destruction, as regards power, of the existing local units of local government. The rural district councils disappear altogether, and the county boroughs, boroughs, urban districts and parishes continue denuded of any powers of any consequence. Whether any persons of any talent will be induced to serve on purely advisory bodies must be open to doubt, and it appears that the continued existence of these comparatively powerless bodies is merely permitted as an attempt to appease existing local interests.

NOTE: In defence of the Commission it must be said that it was faced with a situation where mere tampering with the existing structure was impossible. The need for unification and expansion has had to take pride of place in the interests of the whole future of local government, and to jeopardise this future by retaining unnecessary bodies could not be entertained.

27. Other disadvantages of the recommendations.

(a) *Provincial councils too weak*. It may be argued that insufficient power has been given to the provinces.

NOTE: The Commission obviously intends the unitary authorities to be the focal point of local government and thus confines the more remote provincial council to the provision of the strategic framework in which the operational authorities will work. Thus the power is kept closer to the people. It must also be noted that the powers of the provinces may well be enlarged when the Crowther Commission reports.

(b) *Preference for the city-regions* (*see* **22**(b) and (c) above).

(c) *Personal involvement*. The claims of efficiency, and the advantages of operation on a scale large enough to sustain independence from Whitehall, run counter to the need for a sense of personal involvement in local government.

NOTE: This however must be seen in the light of the wide compromise referred to above (**26**(b)).

(d) *Socialistic character*. The new authorities would take on an increasingly socialistic character, engaging among other things in economic planning, greatly increased council building, and the provision of additional social and economic services.

NOTE: The weight of this criticism is difficult to judge objectively, depending as it does on the subjective views one holds on the role of the state. It may be pointed out that state involvement is a reality and the new structure will possibly reduce criticism in that it places responsibility closer to the electorate.

(e) *Failure to meet reality*. The Commission may be criticised because it fails to meet the main need for reform of local government, in that it imposes too uniform and static a solution which will be outgrown by patterns of movement and settlement.

NOTE: Provision is built into the report for the revision of areas (*see* **8**(f) above). In addition the report has sought a measure of uniformity which, although not desirable in every specific case, is justified on grounds of administrative convenience.

(f) *Research*. It is finally open to criticism because it has failed to implement research which has been carried out on its behalf, and in some cases it is diametrically opposed to such research findings; *e.g.* the obvious and long-accepted effective city-region of the West Riding has not been recommended, and has in fact been split among several different authorities.

IMPLEMENTATION

28. The question of implementation. An obvious question which must be asked is whether or not the Commission will go the way of earlier commissions. Will there be "a brief period of argument followed by a long and probably permanent period of government neglect"? (John Whale, *Sunday Times*.)

29. Obstacles to implementation. Despite an unqualified acceptance of the report by the Prime Minister, the following factors militate against its early implementation:

(*a*) Parliamentary time is too short for legislation under the present government.

(*b*) The Conservative party has reaped the fruits of local election success in recent years. It is likely therefore that, should it form the next government, reform will be low in its priorities for fear of antagonising local party support.

(*c*) Reform will face an exceedingly difficult time in the House of Lords, particularly through strong county representation.

(*d*) Implementation will await the report of the Crowther Commission on constitutional reform which is expected in 1972, as no government would be disposed to make changes which might subsequently have to be revised.

(*e*) Peter Walker, as spokesman for housing and local government for the Opposition, has stated that the Tory party will want full consultation with the authorities and the public.

(*f*) Reform will pose an enormous administrative and legal task; *e.g.* the probable need for rewriting the *Education Act*, 1944.

(*g*) There has already been a strong unfavourable reaction from all the local government associations.

PROGRESS TEST 14

1. Describe the main recommendations of the Redcliffe-Maud Commission. (7–18)

2. What advantages do you consider reform along city-region lines would offer? (22)

3. Discuss the advantages and disadvantages of the Commission's suggested reform. (24–27)

BIBLIOGRAPHY

To acquire a wide basic knowledge of local government, the following additional reading material is suggested.

LEGAL ASPECTS
Cross, *Local Government Law* (Sweet & Maxwell).

FINANCE
Drummond, *The Finance of Local Government* (Allen & Unwin).

HISTORY
Smellie, *A History of Local Government* (Allen & Unwin).

REFORM
The Reports of the Maud and Mallaby Committees (HMSO).
Why Local Democracy? (Fabian Society).
New Life for Local Government (Conservative Political Centre).

GENERAL
Jackson, *Local Government* (Butterworth).
Jackson, *The Machinery of Local Government* (Butterworth).

EXAMINATION TECHNIQUE

Before the examination. It must be emphasised that the key to success in any examination lies in adequate preparation supplemented by constant revision. Preparation may consist of note-making with the emphasis on a clear and logical approach, and must be supplemented by reading from sources as wide as the student's time allows. It is important to prepare for an examination from the beginning of a course, and not to attempt to cram all revision into a few weeks before the actual examination. By spending regular amounts of time on revision during preparation, concentrated revision before the examination with its attendant anxiety and exhaustion can be avoided, and the student will be in a more suitable frame of mind to handle the examination.

At the examination. The following points should be borne in mind during the actual examination:

(a) Read with care the instructions on the examination paper.

(b) Write legibly and use good English.

(c) Read with utmost care the actual examination questions, remembering that marks will be lost for irrelevancy and that valuable time will be wasted.

(d) Spare time to plan in outline each answer and to divide all relevant points into clearly defined paragraphs.

(e) Do not panic if it is felt that excessive time is being spent on a particular question.

(f) Do not write for the sake of writing. It is better to submit a short yet accurate answer, than to resort to the introduction of a large amount of useless information.

These notes are only intended as guidance, and it is appreciated that individuals may have developed their own personal examination techniques which suit them better.

SPECIMEN TEST PAPERS

THE following are used by the kind permission of the Local Government Examinations Board.

Clerical Division Examinations

PAPER 1

Five questions to be answered. Time allowed—3 hours.

1. What is the role of the Parish Council? (Dec. 1964)

2. Describe the main functions of the Clerk of a local authority. (Dec. 1964)

3. Distinguish between the functions of the central department and the local authority in the administration of education. (Dec. 1964)

4. Show how the *Municipal Corporations Act*, 1835, and the *Local Government Act*, 1888, have influenced the structure of local government. (Dec. 1966)

5. Argue the case for *and* the case against the abolition of the aldermanic system. (Dec. 1966)

6. Explain the principles on which properties are assessed for the purposes of the local rate. (Dec. 1966)

7. Describe the main local government services in the sphere of the protection of private property. (June 1967)

8. Which municipal trading powers are most commonly exercised? (Dec. 1966)

9. How does the work of a committee chairman in a local authority differ from that of an ordinary member of a committee? (June 1967)

10. What advantages and disadvantages may be derived from the existence of two or more party organisations in a local council? (June 1967)

PAPER 2

1. What are the chief responsibilities of local authorities in connection with housing? (June 1966)

2. What are the main differences between the powers of a county borough and those of a non-county borough with a population of less than 20,000? (June 1966)

3. "Central control over local authorities has increased, is increasing and ought to be diminished." Discuss this assertion. (June 1966)

4. What are the relative advantages and disadvantages of the general grant? (June 1964)

5. Outline the main functions of *either* an urban district council *or* a rural district council. (June 1964)

6. Write a short account of the functions of any *two* of the following:

    (*a*) the leader of the majority party on a council;

    (*b*) a finance committee;

    (*c*) a medical officer of health. (June 1964)

7. Describe the relationship in local government between chief officers and elected councillors. (Dec. 1965)

8. Outline the duties of the district auditor. (Dec. 1965)

9. Discuss the suggestion that elected members of the larger local authorities should be paid for their services. (Dec. 1965)

10. Give a critical account of the work of the Local Government Commission. (Dec. 1965)

Administrative Examinations
Intermediate

PAPER 1

Five questions to be answered. Time allowed—3 hours.

1. "The main purpose of the district audit is to protect the rate fund from improper expenditure and from the loss of revenue." Have you any criticism of this aim? What are the methods by which it is sought to achieve it? How successful are they? (1965)

2. "The payment of salaries to a limited number of members of large local authorities would enable a local cabinet to develop." Discuss the likelihood and the advantages and disadvantages of such a development. (1965)

3. What are the main ways in which citizens are informed of the activities of their local authority? What improvements can you suggest? (1965)

4. One English city has recently appointed a "manager" in place of a town clerk. Are there any reasons why other local authorities should follow suit? (1966)

5. What factors should be considered in determining the proper boundaries of county boroughs? (1966)

6. "Problems of recruitment and training." Are there such problems in relation to local *councillors*? (1966)

7. "Large local authorities are the most efficient."

"Large local authorities are not *local* at all."

Discuss these views in relation to the reorganisation of local government. (1967)

8. "Politicians and political parties are now very concerned about their 'image'." Describe the "image" of local government today as you see it. (1967)

9. How does a local authority attempt to co-ordinate the work of its various departments, especially in relation to deciding upon priorities for expenditure? (1967)

10. Outline the main changes in the structure of local government which have taken place in the twentieth century. (1967)

PAPER 2

1. What were the purposes of either:

(a) The *Local Government Acts*, 1888 and 1894.

or

(b) The *Local Government Acts*, 1919 and 1933? (1965)

2. Describe the rate deficiency grant and discuss its efficacy in the system of Exchequer aid to local authorities. (1965)

3. "Local democracy can be saved only by regionalism." "Regionalism can be neither democratic nor local."
Discuss these views. (1966)

4. Is there a danger of departmentalism in the organisation of local authorities? If so, how is it best met? (1966)

5. What changes in local government finance have been introduced by the present Labour Government? (1967)

6. "A town and country planner need not be an architect, a sociologist, an economist, or a statistician: he must be a visionary."
Comment on this assessment. (1967)

7. Why does the central government exert influence over the actions of local authorities? (1968)

8. Why is the rating system widely regarded as unsatisfactory? (1968)

9. Which single Act of Parliament has had the greatest effect on the development of our local government system? Explain fully the reasons for your choice. (1968)

10. Consider how far decisions on council business should be delegated:

(a) to committees,

(b) to chief officers. (1968)

INDEX